MICHAEL S. SMITH ELEMENTS OF STYLE

Michael S. Smith

Elements of Style

With Diane Dorrans Saeks

RIZZOLI
NEW YORK

First published in the United States of America in 2005
by Rizzoli International Publications, Inc.
300 Park Avenue South
New York, NY 10010
www.rizzoliusa.com

2006 2007 2008 / 10 9 8 7 6 5 4 3

Printed in China

ISBN-10:0-8478-2762-3
ISBN-13:987-0-8478-2762-6

Library of Congress Cataloging-in-Publication Data

Smith, Michael, 1964-
Michael Smith: elements of style/with Diane Dorrans Saeks.–
1st American ed.
p. cm.
ISBN 0-8478-2762-3 (hardcover: alk. paper)
1. Smith, Michael, 1964—Themes, motives. 2. Interior decoration–United
States–History–20th century. 3. Interior decoration. I. Title: Elements of
style. II. Saeks, Diane Dorrans. III. Title.
NK2004.3.S63 2005
747'.092--dc22
2005011547

Designed by Subtitle

Opposite: A handsome pair of Labradors at the Los Angeles house of producer Donna Arkoff Roth.

Previous page: In a thirtieth-floor apartment in the Carlyle tower, a Gandharan head balances on a marble-topped gessoed and gilded table. A Winslow Homer pen-and-ink seascape floats above them. The floor is bleached English oak parquet.

Following page: In Peter Morton's Los Angeles house, a Brice Marden painting hovers above a Jean Prouvé table. The décor is controlled and the colors subdued, in deference to the classic painting. The mid-twentieth-century industrial materials and engineering of the table stand in fine juxtaposition with the traditional style of the chair.

CONTENTS

PREFACE
By Diane Dorrans Saeks

"Hi, I'm on my way to the airport. I'll call you the moment I arrive in London," said Michael Smith early one winter morning. And so we began work on this new book, much of it conducted by telephone. Travel and long-distance communications delineate decorators' and writers' worlds, and this conversational modus operandi was a revealing and improvisational way to write our book together.

Over months, we discussed all aspects of design. We'd meet in Los Angeles and San Francisco, then continue the dialogue via cell phone from distant hotel suites and noisy restaurants, from Paris, Antwerp, Montana, Santa Barbara, Woodside, and Jamaica. He'd call from his Range Rover, navigating the labyrinth of roads in Malibu.

"I'm totally involved in fulfilling my clients' needs and wishes and that requires travel," said the designer, touring Maastricht. "I take clients to Paris or London to find the best antiques, paintings, textiles. Viewing art and antiques, we also encounter the best original interiors, make the rounds of antiquaires or workshops. I gather inspiration, make new discoveries, sense the zeitgeist. It's important for a decorator to be incredibly alert, to look ahead, and to stay curious and remain open-minded."

His mission is to keep learning.

"I've just arrived in Paris, and I'll call you as soon as I get to the hotel," Michael Smith said. A conversation on creating mood continued as the designer wrapped himself in Etro scarves against the winter chill and set off for a visit with antiquaire Ariane Dandois. During a brisk walk along the rue Jacob to the quai Voltaire we talked about color.

For Michael Smith, custom design is a passionate search for beauty, and a full-on immersion process. Saturday mornings, he's at home working his way through sixteen new auction catalogs. Sundays anywhere in the world he's looking at real estate, viewing houses for sale, imagining living in this London or Paris pied-a-terre.

The influences of design history, the best of classicism and modernism, and quirky twentieth-century detours of design, are all refined, adapted, tweaked, refreshed and filtered through Michael Smith's superbly attuned knowledge of design history, and his sense of balance, mood, proportion and theatricality.

In *The Decoration of Houses*, Edith Wharton and Ogden Codman noted, "Proportion is . . . something, indefinable to the unprofessional eye, which gives repose and distinction to a room, in its effects as intangible as that all-pervading essence which the ancients called soul."

Michael Smith was born with a perfect pitch for proportion.

"My work is about the pursuit of many ideas, for the pleasure and enjoyment of my clients," he said. "I do the unexpected, avoid trends and fashion, and I never repeat myself. Style is hard to pinpoint precisely, but for me it always revolves around individuality. It's often reductive, and may involve a dash of eccentricity, quirkiness and exaggeration."

In his interiors, there are no radical rooms or design statements. Rather, his fine-tuned examination of the best of design, art, and antiques, and his intuitive understanding of architecture result in rooms that exude perfect calm and poise, a portrait of his clients.

Some rooms derive their glamour from one seductive and memorable move—hundreds of yards of white linen curtains, for example. Unafraid of plainness, simplicity, or modesty, he deliberately underplays his hand, covering wood floors with great old rugs that are charming but not especially precious, and accompanying a pair of smooth old leather club chairs with a scuffed low table (Chinese, probably) that shows it age in the most reassuring way.

"I've always believed in the romantic concept of individuality," he said. "The point is to make your point with confidence. I would never say, "I'm going to make beautiful rooms and I dare you to live in them." I imagine my clients sitting in front of the fire, or drawing the curtains, or reading on a linen velvet-covered sofa. I create great moments for them, but I don't treat my clients like actors on a stage."

Working in a dazzling variety of styles, the designer acknowledges but is not bound to design history nor the long-ago beauty of historical interiors. There is no nostalgia. Influences are there but his is always a virtuoso expression. Importantly, the décor is appropriate to the architecture, the location, and the spirit of the owners.

Even as he embarked on his design career, in his early twenties, Michael Smith rejected the concept of the signature

---

Defining Moment *Opposite:* In the New York City river-view residence of the de Rothschild family, an eighteenth-century English marble mantelpiece makes a perfect perch for an elegant Cambodian figure, circa twelfth century. Accompanying the delicately sculpted torso is a Piero Manzoni kaolin on canvas, *Achrome*, circa 1959. The design concept here: subtle, understated, transcendent of trends.

style that was then all the rage.

"What is your style?" is a question he answers with politeness, but it's one that baffles him. His work is directed by the location, the specific clients, the architecture, climate, light, timing, the decade.

Michael Smith has drawn on historical Portuguese interiors, admires the interiors of Edwin Lutyens' great country houses, and looks on Andrea Palladio and Renzo Mongiardino as mentors. Inspiration may be found in Axel Vervoordt's famous castle residence and his Kanaal headquarters, in sixteenth-century Flemish interiors, twenties New York architecture, great English drawing rooms, or thirties Paris salons.

As the sixteenth-century Venetian painter Tintoretto wrote on a sign on his studio door, "Drawing by Michelangelo, color by Titian." Every artist or designer does well to know design history and to draw from the well of creativity.

Michael Smith's approach to luxury advocates simplicity, and often prescribes creamy, timeless colors like ivory, sage, and taupe. Draperies, simple and untrimmed, may be made of a matte taffeta, linen cotton, or super-luxe cream wool suiting. No pattern or mishandled color breaks the calm mood. The decor looks as if it has evolved over decades, not months.

In a recent interior, he had the walls crafted in Italian plaster, handwaxed in a pale creamy color that seems to change subtly with the light as day fades into night. It's the best kind of luxury, somewhat hidden, visible only to an eye that is finely tuned to color nuances.

Perhaps the ultimate luxury is working with Michael Smith.

Design Versatility *Above and Opposite:* Michael Smith tunes each of his interiors to his clients' personalities, dreams, aspirations, and lives. His design concepts may take a chinoiserie direction, with lacquered and gilded cabinets and exquisite ceramics and finishes. One easy design trap he avoids, however, is theme design, in which every aspect of a room hews to a specific prepackaged design idea. In this handsome timbered living room, a light-hearted chandelier hovers above a somewhat traditional grouping of sofas and chairs. The designer keeps the finished décor inviting, timeless, and fresh with pale colors, antique textiles, bold bookcases, and an individual mix of antiques and new pieces.

FOREWORD
By Howard Marks

My wife Nancy and I first met Michael Smith in September 1993, when we asked him over to discuss a house we'd bought in Montecito. "Bounded in" is how we think of it, and yet he obviously didn't leap into our house physically. The bound came from his energy, enthusiasm, and excitement. "I saw this room in *AD!*" he said. "It's great! And didn't you wait a year for the fabric?"

He was right about the fabric, and ever since we've wondered how he remembered one fabric—and the interminable year we spent waiting for it—from the hundreds of houses that appeared in print every year. With that lone sentence Michael had displayed his eye for detail, his photographic memory, and his consuming interest in decoration.

We drove together to Montecito to see the house, which was what Michael would call a "style-free" remodel built on the foundation of the original house constructed in 1894 by Mrs. Pillsbury. Michael could have taken the easy way out: an Italianate or Mediterranean villa, like so many in the area. But he didn't. "Portuguese!" he said immediately. "It'll be great! Because Portugal owned colonies all over the world, like Goa and Brazil, its style is different, quirky, and eclectic." And these characteristics can be seen in each of Michael's projects—if the client is smart enough to let him have his way.

What else defines his work? If you're after "magnificent," "splendid," or "impressive," Michael's probably not the decorator for you. He's more likely to give you "playful" than "serious." And while it will cost a lot, it won't wear its price tag on its sleeve.

Historical references are everywhere—but history is never followed slavishly. His houses look comfortable and timeworn even when new, and the contents go together like old friends—but they're never museum-like or stale. To borrow from Michael's personal vocabulary, the contents are neither "matchy-matchy" (at one end of the coordination spectrum) nor "random" (at the other).

In each room there's likely to be something that doesn't quite fit, one piece from a different style or era, one splash of color that doesn't match or conform, but it all goes together beautifully. It's decorating that doesn't take itself too seriously and appears effortless—like its author.

The key ingredient in each project is the unique inspiration Michael brings to it. When we found our Los Angeles residence in 1996, the vision came right off the tip of his tongue. "It was built in 1939 as 'Hollywood regency': the cinematic, southern California take on 1780–1840 English architecture. Let's put it back that way!" And so he went on to add architectural details, furniture, and colors based on

---

Youthful Classicism *Opposite:* In Bel Air, Michael Smith orchestrated an updated traditional interior with contemporary paintings, black and white photography, and pale walls with a hint of color and warmth. White walls here would have been so expected—and would have added nothing to the vivacious mix.

that style, combined with French and Asian elements. He walked in a few days later with a fabric sample. "I've always wanted to find the right use for this; it'll be perfect for the master bedroom walls!" And it was. We hated the balustrades, and he replaced them with a design from Sir John Soane's house circa 1822: also perfect.

Now we've traded the Montecito house for a new project in Malibu. The house we bought might be described as "traditional," but its design and details were in no way faithful to classical architecture (not to mention that it had a formality we didn't want at the beach). Michael immediately proposed "seventeenth-century loft living" as the guiding inspiration, and we were intrigued. We soon flew to Antwerp to see the exciting fusion of old and new being applied in northern European decorating. The architecture needed improvement, and Michael suggested the style of Andrea Palladio, the leading architect of Italy's Veneto region in the sixteenth century. We visited Vicenza to see Palladio's

symmetrical buildings in their native setting, and London to see Chiswick, the epitome of English Palladianism. Michael's lightning-bolt idea this time: "Pietra serena, the local stone with which Florence is paved—nothing else will do for the floors!"

Portugal in Montecito, Hollywood Regency, Antwerp loft living—sometimes we can't even hold in our heads the vision of what the final house is supposed to look like. And yet the result is always remarkable: We get exactly what we want in terms of aesthetics and livability. We get houses whose beauty never stops amazing us. And we have fun in the process, and invariably regret the project's end.

Updated Traditional *Above and Opposite:* Michael Smith notes that while he can work in any style or design approach, his clients like the comfort, familiarity, timelessness, and ease of traditional décor. Los Angeles clients, to the surprise of many design observers, are not trend-hopping style slaves. As shown in these new interiors, the designer is adept at fashioning rooms that mix antiques, modern art, contemporary crafts, and furniture with pedigrees for his Southern California clients. He avoids an "all-English", or "all-French" look by mixing rare, quirky, and unexpected pieces and bringing in some of his own furniture and accessory designs for balance.

INTRODUCTION
By Krista Smith

I met Michael Smith shortly after I moved to Los Angeles. He was charming and incredibly funny, with a laserlike precision on almost every subject, and I immediately realized this was someone I must get to know. Almost a decade later, that first impression has proven accurate. Michael has consistently managed to achieve the perfect blend of casual elegance for his illustrious clientele of rock icons, movie stars, royals, and international tycoons. And he has the rare quality of being equally at home everywhere from a townhouse in New York to a mansion in Malibu, an English country estate, or a G5 jet airplane. No other contemporary decorator has cast such a wide and influential net.

According to Michael, his goal for the book was simple: "I wanted to demystify decorating. I think that one of my worst habits is that I tend to forget to explain the reason I do things." While there are certainly parallels between finishing a house and finishing a book, it helps to have a great writer on board when you're attempting the latter, and Michael found the perfect collaborator in Diane Dorrans Saeks: "She's been friends with so many of the great California decorators, like John Dickinson and Michael Taylor, and she's written about them all." Michael and Diane have known each other for more than fifteen years, so it was a seamless union.

Thumbing through these exquisite pages, one can clearly see that Michael is not just a decorator for hire but a devoted disciple of architecture and history. He pays homage to both disciplines in every project, but he also admits to a visceral love of furniture and of fabric. He likes being involved in every stage of a new space's development, "from finding the ground to designing the stationery, to buying the towels, to planning the garden."

The actress Michelle Pfeiffer has been a loyal client of Michael's over the course of ten years and five houses, although she didn't plan it that way. "I called him to basically do one room for me," she says. "It was my living room, and I said, 'I like everything else in my house, and I like many things in this room. I just need you to help me pull it all together.' Well, needless to say, within a year the only thing that remained of my original furniture in the entire house was my dining room table."

It is rare in any field to have a business relationship that spans more than a decade, but it's especially so in interior design, where the rush is always on to find the latest fad. Michael, however, much like the legendary interior decorator Billy Haines, has stayed with clients even as they've cycled through new husbands, wives, and climates. Dominick Dunne, *Vanity Fair* columnist and bestselling

---

Timeless Design *Opposite:* Leather club chairs, an antique English occasional table, simple monochromatic window coverings, pillows made from vintage fabrics, an urn-shaped lamp, garden flowers: This was Michael Smith's recipe for these Los Angeles interiors he designed more than fifteen years ago, when he first began his design company. It's a timeless, classic approach that works well on the West Coast, the East Coast, and every location in between. This flexible plan allows for easy additions and updates, and it's practical and functional. Interior design, said Smith, should be planned from the start so that it can evolve as a family's requirements, tastes, and furniture and art collections change and grow.

novelist, remembers, "In my era of Hollywood living, which began in the late fifties, I was fortunate enough to see up close the last glamorous period of beautiful people living beautifully. I was under contract to 20th Century Fox when Marilyn Monroe was the queen of the lot. There was a real elegance to everyday life . . . for years at-home glamour went out of style; I always felt it was the Sharon Tate murders in Beverly Hills that changed the way people lived. Looking at these lovely pictures of Michael Smith's magical interiors, I see that he is bringing glamour back, suited to a new era that he understands in the ways that Billy Haines understood his era."

Michael's greatest joy comes from poring over auction catalogs and hunting down antiques—a passion that places him on an airplane at least once every ten days. "I sometimes go through twelve to fourteen auction catalogs in a weekend, the way people go through scripts," he says. "It's exciting for me, the possibility of finding the perfect thing that fits perfectly. Those things are drops from heaven." For me, those "drops from heaven" came when Michael took one quick look around my home in the Hollywood Hills and a week later a truck arrived with the most exquisite Japanese floral antique screened panels, along with an Italian painting of Naples that hung perfectly in an awkward space. Even the rugs he brought fit the space impeccably, all without measuring an inch.

The result of this hunting-and-gathering approach is that, as Pfeiffer says, no two of his houses are the same; there is no signature look or museumlike stiffness. Even when there are Picassos and Monets hanging on the walls, the comfort of the room seduces you.

Michael always knew what he wanted to do, and his work today retains the distinctive flavor of the place where he grew up: Newport Beach, California—in the heart of Orange County, home to John Wayne airport and a coastal enclave of wealth. After high school, he headed to New York to attend the prestigious Otis Institute, now the Parsons School of Design, where today he is the only alumnus on the board of trustees. A voracious reader, he consumed heavy-duty history books as if they were dime-store romances. "I would read everything there was about Japan," he says, "and then I would go on to Russia." (One of the things that makes Michael one of the best dinner companions on either coast is that he knows something about everything.)

After an inspirational year abroad in London, Michael was hired by the famed New York decorator John Saladino. In 1993, almost immediately after returning to Los Angeles, he started working with clients in the entertainment industry. He met Cindy Crawford, who was decorating a house with her then-husband Richard Gere. "I had never had a decorator or anything like that," Crawford says. "But we just clicked from the very beginning. I loved that he was my age—he was an equal and we have the same references. Michael doesn't fake anything. He is contemporary, he's hip, and he knows what's happening, but his foundation is always flawless because he knows what's right from a historical and architectural point of view."

In 2005, Michael completed work on the New York apartment of Lady Lynn de Rothschild, wife of Sir Evelyn. Lady de Rothschild described how she came to work with Michael. "I was in the shop of a fantastic London antique dealer and I said I was looking for someone who I could work with who would give me something that didn't look like every apartment on Park Avenue. His words were: The person who most regularly buys my best things is Michael Smith. So I called Michael and we got along immediately. He has fantastic taste and a fantastic ability to translate what you want into reality."

Peter Morton, another longtime client and the owner of Morton's restaurant in West Hollywood and the Hard Rock Hotel and Casino in Las Vegas, is grateful to Michael for urging him to buy pieces by Jean Prouvé, the French architect and furniture maker, "when no one knew who Prouvé was." For Morton, the secret to this extraordinary decorator's success is obvious: "Michael is always ahead of the curve."

The Art of Placement *Opposite:* In the living room of his former Bel-Air house, Smith seduces the eye with orchids in terra-cotta pots, a nineteenth-century copy of a Grecian urn, favorite books, and a Han horse, all on a marble-topped Kentian table. The painting is by Beatrice Caracciolo.

Michael S. Smith
The Interiors

Michael Smith has often said that he is intrigued by the romantic idea of individuality of rooms, and the specific voice and demeanor of each piece of furniture. His fascination with creating each room anew, and with making every interior a perfect fit—perhaps a provocative fit—for each client drives him ever forward.

Rejecting a clichéd signature look since the very first day of his two-decade career, he creates rooms that seduce—quietly. These are houses where dogs and kids and creative people passionate about social and political causes can congregate. These are also sunny suites and romantic corners where a couple can be alone together in tranquil bliss. The completed décor is often understated and a little spare, and never uptight, wisely leaving room for people and their books and their new collections of art, antiques, and beautiful things added over time.

Perhaps best of all, Michael Smith applies both romance and logic to his designs. "I love Chinese wallpaper in dining rooms," he said. "It's very addictive because the color, detail, romance, and intricacy are magical and entrancing in the daytime, and especially at night. It's like a special effect in a candlelit room. It's theatrical and dimensional, and it's practical. A splash of wine, a dash of champagne, are never going to show among the beautiful details of the design."

His work for clients is about perfecting, perfecting, and perfecting the architecture, the floors, the walls, the background, so that the furniture and art can be arranged in a natural and seemingly offhand, unforced manner.

He travels from New York to Paris, Antwerp, Round Hill, Paris, and Malibu throughout the year, season to season, effortlessly dressed in Levi's jeans, Anderson & Shephard Scottish tweed blazers or an Arnys La Forestiere jacket (modified from a Sologne gamekeeper's jacket by Le Corbusier and worn by Picasso, Cocteau, and Sartre), and Lobb brown riding boots or Clark's suede desert boots, and Etro or Charvet cotton shirts.

He is at home in beach bungalows, Hollywood Hills mansions, Montecito quintas, Manhattan penthouses, Antwerp lofts, and Paris's most snooty antiquaries. The point is to observe, to learn, to gather new friendships, to educate both himself and his clients.

Many of his clients have gathered museum-quality art collections. "I've hung Picasso paintings on a stenciled geometric paper because it give the painting more importance and it stands out strongly in relief," he said. "Rather than add visual noise, wallpaper, well chosen, can unify dissimilar elements and give quietness and grace to rooms."

Logic, practicality, and romance, surely that combination is the Michael Smith signature.

Composed Comfort *Opposite:* The beautifully balanced and calm interior of Donna Roth's beach house is achieved with a tonally even color scheme. In this room, décor, flowers, lighting, and accessories are relaxed and understated, perfect for a beach house.

SERENE INTERIORS, RIVER VIEWS

On the Eastern edge of Manhattan overlooking a broad stretch of the placid East River stands palatial River House. Here, shaded by noble old trees and sheltered from the noise of crosstown traffic, live some of the most high-profile names and storied families of New York. But this is a private retreat, with the luxury of graciously proportioned interiors, the ornamentation of cornices, pilasters, and pediments, and the added pleasures of reflected light and dazzling city panoramas. There, business executive Lynn Forester acquired a duplex apartment with graceful staircases, marble floors, elegant detailing, and views on all four sides. It is the quintessential "grand apartment." When she later married Sir Evelyn de Rothschild (and became Lady Lynn de Rothschild) she decided to make it a great family home, without the opulence that might be expected of the building and without taking on "le style Rothschild," the lush and luxuriant décor favored by the family in Paris and London.

Starting with cans and cans of "good Jeffersonian white paint" to give the woodwork new life, the walls of the living room and adjoining rooms were freshened with pale gray Venetian plaster. Upholstered chairs and sofas are down-filled in the traditional manner, but there is nothing overstated or grandiose about their proportions. The art is stimulating and provocative without being oppressive. The effect is calm, peaceful, and serene.

State of Grace: *Above and Opposite:* In the de Rothschild living room, an early-nineteenth-century German commode and a Georgian mirror (both from Carlton Hobbs, London) contrast with a pair of Giacometti stools. Above the 18th-century English marble chimneypiece hangs Piero Manzoni's *Achrome*, kaolin on canvas, circa 1959. The Cambodian figures date from the twelfth century.

Setting for Lively Conversation *Following pages:* The dining room walls are covered in an 18th-century Chinese wallpaper that takes on a magical quality in the evening. The antique mahogany table is from the London antiquarian Christopher Hodsoll. The George I–style gilt chairs are covered in sage silk velvet from the Silk Trading Co.

The plan for the de Rothschild apartment was to craft rooms that felt comfortable and stylish. They would need a certain flexibility to serve as a background for entertaining and family life. It would be reductive, editing out the previous owner's damasks, rich silks, and heavy velvets, and creating rooms that belong to the twenty-first century. The soft celadon, silver, cream, and white tones selected also serve as an understated canvas for a burgeoning collection of museum-quality furniture by Jacques-Emile Ruhlmann and Diego Giacometti, as well as works by artists, including Agnes Martin, Giorgio Morandi, Luc Tuymans, Robert Ryman, Ellsworth Kelly, Robert Rauschenberg, and Jackson Pollock. They are balanced by silk carpets, antique marble floors, and even a dark green leather floor in the family room.

Tone on Tone *Above:* In the library, walls are covered in a silk and linen fabric traditionally used for men's suiting. The window shades are eighteenth-century Japanese with a subtle edging of Indian sari silk. The antique chairs were acquired in London. The sofa is upholstered in a textile by Lelièvre.

Sunshine Day *Opposite:* In the sitting room adjacent to the living room, a 2002 oil on canvas by Robert Ryman stands on a demi-lune table. The marble pedestal table is from Quatrain, Los Angeles.

The art of the décor in this stately apartment is that while the furniture and art are all new to these rooms, there is no feeling of "instant decoration." The mix of antiques and modern art, and the collection of rare carpets and dazzling objects are luxurious with an air of old-world taste, but they feel perfectly at home, as if the family had merely added and freshened up an already stunning residence.

The plan from the start was to keep it youthful and fresh, without the obvious trappings of luxury and opulence. Books are stacked on tables and desks, and each room is arranged with chairs and tables that invite family gatherings and conversation.

In the meantime, the de Rothschilds divide their time between New York and London, where they enjoy a Chelsea residence that formerly belonged to the great painter and watercolorist, John Singer Sargent. Peace and comfort reign there, too, just as they do in their East River retreat.

Water, Water *Above:* The glamorous bathroom was planned with luxury in mind. The handheld shower and whirlpool bath are from the Michael Smith For Town collection for Kallista. On the gleaming marble floor, the Jules Leleu chair is from Maison Gerard.

Modern Glamour *Right:* The bedroom walls are upholstered in Sargent Silk from Cowtan & Tout, and the curtains are made of Bennison's Damask Rose on beige silk. The bed is sheathed in shagreen.

A CERTAIN PERFECTION

James E. Dolena (1888–1978) was considered one of the best classical architects practicing in Los Angeles in the thirties, forties, and fifties, and he has an insider following today among those who are connoisseurs of the estates and residences in Beverly Hills. Dolena, who was born in St. Petersburg, Russia, arrived in Los Angeles with his colleague, the Canadian artist H. Valentine Fanshaw, to install a mural in a public building. Over the following two decades, Dolena built some of the most elegant houses in Bel-Air, and he

subsequently became known as the "architect to the stars."

This elegant, beautifully proportioned house was built by Dolena in the early thirties. Positioned on a knoll on three acres of landscaped gardens, it has views of the silvery Pacific Ocean in the distance. T.H. Robsjohn-Gibbings was one of its earliest decorators, and Johnny Weissmuller and Tito Jackson are among its previous owners. Still, for all its pedigree, this was to be a worldly but very relaxed and comfortable family home for Howard and Nancy Marks.

Lasting Impression *Above and Opposite:* The living room of the Bel-Air house has large bay windows with a view of the pool and gardens, and all-day sunlight. The Marks have made more than a dozen trips to Europe with Michael Smith, and have assembled a notable collection of European, Asian, and American antique furniture, art, and fine decorative objects. The voluminous curtains, which add a joyful punctuation of color around the room, are layered with Prima Seta's Lemon Ice and Imperial Yellow silk. To counterbalance the opulence of the matte silk, the curtain hardware is deliberately understated, with only the smallest finials. The gilt Chippendale chairs are upholstered in Claremont's Faille Jaspe Stripe silk. The bookcase was formerly in the private dining room of revered Paris antiques dealer/decorator, Madeleine Castaing, who kept only the best antiques for herself.

Smith's concept for the interior of the house was inspired by visits to the great English country houses, in which centuries of art collections and antiques come together in an inviting manner. The design would be a bit loose, so that the Chinese tables, Gandharan Buddhas, Hepplewhite chairs, and Roman torso sculptures would appear to have been gathered over generations. In fact, it took ten or twelve trips to Paris, Brussels, London, and New York and dedicated auction sleuthing around the world to gather the beautiful collections of blue-and-white Chinese pottery, Greek urns, antique textiles, and even the Swedish chandelier, found at Florian Papp, Inc., New York.

Architect Oscar Shamamian, of Ferguson & Shamamian, added a Sir John Soane–inspired classical staircase, as well as French doors that open to the garden and the pool. Over the seven decades of its life span, the house has also gained a number of outbuildings, along with an underground squash court, and a whimsical folly of a pool house.

The Discerning Eye *Above and Opposite:* A series of well-researched visits to Paris and New York in search of exquisite furniture also resulted in a notable collection of rugs. In the study, a nineteenth-century Bessarabian, found at a Sotheby's auction, sets an Orientalist motif. The sofa, designed by Michael Smith, is covered in silk velvet. Collections of objects on tables and desks have a classical Grand Tour focus.

Chinoiserie Dream *Above and Opposite:* The carved and gilt console table in the dining room was a treasure from the classical Irish residence Luttrellstown Castle. On its marble top, stand a trio of temples carved in soapstone, from the Michael Taylor estate sale. Vintage chinoiserie wallpaper and a towering giltwood Chinese pagoda bestow an escapist mood in the dining room. Moss green curtains backed with a paler silk are crafted from Prima Seta's Nuit silk.

Perchance to Dream *Above, Opposite, and Overleaf:* Bedroom design is the forte of Michael Smith, who lavishes attention on four-poster beds and bedroom walls. The original inspiration for the Chinese bed in the guest room is the glamorous carved Badminton House bed, now in the Victoria and Albert Museum in London. (Chairs from this Chinese bedroom set are in the collections of the museum and of Ann and Gordon Getty of San Francisco.) Walls are covered in blue-and-white printed cotton in the Cimarosa pattern by Fortuny. In the principal bedroom, the walls are covered in Montaigne fabric from Cowtan & Tout. The four-poster bed, by Sotheby's Restoration, has a canopy of blue-gray silk lined in green and beige silk.

PASSAGE TO PORTUGAL

When longtime clients acquired an eight-acre property in Montecito, near Santa Barbara, they walked the land with Michael Smith to get to know it before making decisions on the new residence that would be built there.

Among the centuries-old native oaks was an 1890s Mission Revival house that had been aggressively remodeled in the seventies. It had the sadly dated aspect of a tract house, was poorly situated, and had no character or charm.

"The estate is on a gentle hillside in the most beautiful part of Montecito," said Smith. "It has views to the Pacific Ocean, and groves of olive trees. We wanted to build a house that looked as if it had been there for a century, and was part of the history of the land."

On a hot, dry summer day this very private property has such a sense of calm it could be in a remote corner of the Iberian Peninsula. The scent of lavender and jasmine spins in the warm air, and the soothing splash of fountains, the buzz of bees and crickets in the olive trees, even the noon bells of a nearby church suggest Portugal rather than Southern California.

Travels to Sintra *Above:* In preparation for the design of the Portuguese Colonial-inspired house in Montecito, Michael Smith and his clients traveled to fabled Sintra, Cascais, and the Douro Valley in Portugal to visit noted quintas and historic houses in their original glory. This was not intended to be a slavish copy, nor a reproduction, but they were searching for the spirit, the essence, and the best of Portuguese country design. "I wanted this house to have signature details—the tiled walls—but to be somewhat quirky and rustic, not dolled-up," said Smith. *Opposite:* The adjacent library, with bookcases of cherrywood, has a limestone fireplace.

Working with architects Tichenor & Thorp, Smith created a new vision and history for the property.

"Almost immediately we were inspired to build a new house based on a Portuguese quinta," said Smith. "I researched Portuguese traditional architecture. My clients and I flew to Lisbon and explored the Douro Valley to visit historic country houses, and to view in-depth the materials, the ornamentation, the rationale of the architecture, the color palette, and the textures and décor."

Smith also observed the country interiors, which tend to be spare, calm, and furnished from around the globe with handcrafted chairs, hand-carved beds, and noble paintings of long-forgotten ancestors.

Planning a Portuguese quinta (a traditional manor house) in Montecito, Smith was immediately aware that he would have great latitude for creative expression in both the exteriors and the interiors.

The quinta traditionally afforded a broader aesthetic because Portugal at various points in the fifteenth, sixteenth, and seventeenth centuries ruled a trading empire that spanned the globe, from Africa and India to China and Brazil. These rich equatorial additions to the Portuguese design vocabulary gave endless possibilities for exotic textiles, eccentric furniture, colorful paintings, and quirky hand-blocked fabrics.

A Study in Balance and Harmony *Opposite:* For the dining room, Michael Smith found antique Portuguese colonial chairs in Lisbon and commissioned a dozen superb copies (antique chairs seldom come in groups of fourteen all in fine condition). Blue-and-white Chinese export plates, on the wall, were made for the Portuguese market.

Dreaming in Style *Above:* Portuguese floral chintz found in Lisbon was used for the walls, curtains, and bedcoverings. The carpet is English needlepoint.

Portugal Idealized *Following pages:* Michael Smith traveled throughout Portugal to gain an understanding of the style, textures, and traditions of its quintas and palaces. For this Montecito retreat, he commissioned a California tile company to custom-make a series of blue and white tiles for a cooling effect on the sitting room.

In order to make the new quinta look old, Smith and Tichenor & Thorp drew up a one-level rambling house that included terraces, quiet courtyards, enclosed pools, fountains, and views framed by oaks and olive trees.

"When you're translating traditional architecture, it's essential to borrow in a way that's not tricky or museum-like," he said. "We wanted architecture that felt sophisticated and polished, but was not heavy-handed or picturesque. It was important that the house should feel like California, and not imposed on the landscape. It had to feel authentic."

The color palette selected for both the interior and the exterior was simple and reductive.

"When we were in Portugal, we were drawn to the traditional azulejos, the ornamental blue-and-white tiles that seem to be on every house there," said Smith. "We went to the National Tile Museum in Lisbon to study the many historic styles and designs. Then we brought our favorite tiles home to California and had them copied in a factory near Los Angeles. We captured the old traditional pale indigo blue in a series of geometric patterns."

The tiles make rooms feel cool and restful on hot afternoons, and they are also practical for a country house.

"I used the tiles as they're used in manor houses in Portugal, on the walls as a patterned wainscot," said Smith. He also had scenic tiles painted, and they were placed on walls and around courtyards, in the Portuguese style.

Muted Light of Summer *Opposite:* An antique Portuguese table in rosewood greets guests who arrive at the Montecito house, at the end of a long driveway. The antique antlers, naturally shed, were found in the South of France. *Above:* The pair of sofas were covered in white-on-white embroidered cotton/linen fabric. Ethereal light shimmers in this bedroom/sitting room, which opens onto a terrace. An antique gilt mirror gleams with light, and further enhances the lighter-than-air quality of the room.

A WORLDLY VIEW AT LAS ENCINITAS

This estate in Montecito is one of the most private—and privileged—in a region known for its opulence.

Sequestered behind a series of tall handcrafted iron gates and reached by a driveway that traverses century-old stone bridges, the house seems far from civilization. It is situated among the glades of gnarled coastal oaks that inspired its name, Las Encinitas. Native oaks thrive in this sunny climate, and the property speaks of quiet luxury to the family and their guests.

Michael Smith worked with architects Tichenor & Thorp, along with Ferguson & Shamamian, on the manor house, and at the same time planned a series of guest-houses and a pool house in the Portuguese country style that would look as if they had stood there since California was first settled.

"The main house required a certain formality in its execution, but with the outbuildings, I was able to be a bit more eccentric," said the designer. "We followed the same motifs of mullioned windows, blue-and-white Portuguese tiles, stone fireplaces, and terra-cotta–tile floors, but the decorating is much looser and more theatrical."

Country Bliss *Above and Opposite:* The new guesthouse is curtained with rambling roses and wreathed with old native oaks and manzanita trees. The oaks, which are deciduous, provide clouds of shade on summer afternoons. The new water garden (which looks as if it has been there for a century) offers perfect tranquility and splendor in the late afternoon. The canvas tent was custom crafted in the traditional manner by the Jaipur workshops initiated by the Maharajah of Jaipur. Ceremonial cotton tents, in the grand traditional manner, are an Indian specialty.

The late, great Italian decorator/set designer Renzo Mongiardino has always been one of Michael Smith's favorites. It was to Mongiardino's legendary interiors that Smith turned for inspiration for the guest suites of Las Encinitas.

One of Mongiardino's favorite ploys in the seventies was to tent rooms (as he did at the Palazzo Brandolini in Venice) in hundreds of yards of hand-blocked Indian fabrics. It is a dramatic move, and Smith replicated the luxurious look with two hundred Indian bedspreads from Urban Outfitters (a longtime design source) glued to the guesthouse walls and ceiling. Bordered curtains in the same natural cream, ocher, blackberry, and sepia tones hang from simple rods. As a counterpoint, there is also striped ticking by Pierre Frey.

In London, Paris, and Lisbon, Smith found antique Goanese tables inset with mother-of-pearl, blue-and-white Chinese pottery urns that he converted into lamps, flat-weave Turkish carpets, an Indo-Portuguese four-poster bed, *verre eglomise* paintings, and a painted Moorish chair.

"The point was to make the rooms look as if they'd evolved over decades, rather than come together over a short period of time," said Smith. "There's nothing more tragic than rooms that look as if the furniture all arrived on the same day, in the same truck."

Guest suites, said the designer, should be an escape from the everyday. "It's fun to have décor that's eccentric, exotic, and special," he said. "But I also pay special attention to great mattresses and all the creature comforts in guest suites. Friends and family should have places to relax, read, and nap after a long day of tennis and swimming."

During the three-year project, Smith was involved with every aspect of creating Las Encinitas. While Los Angeles landscape designer Mia Lehrer worked on the romantic, fragrant gardens, Smith was obsessing about the right gravel for the driveway, the correct mortar color, and the perfect tone for window frames and doors. At the same time, he and his clients were also selecting every piece of outdoor furniture, and the ornamental urns and statuary that decorate the courtyards, an allée of wisteria, walks, rose gardens, and the fruit orchard.

"It was a brilliant collaboration and everything came together so beautifully," said Smith. "Now, design magazine editors and my clients' guests and neighbors tell me it is their favorite house."

The house seems at home among the oaks, and it has a very relaxed feeling. It is a wonderful refuge. When the gates close behind you and you head up the driveway, you are in another world.

Summer Pleasures *Opposite and Right:* The bedrooms of the Montecito guest quarters open onto the private garden and a corridor of old native oak trees. The painted antique Venetian bedposts were found in Venice and custom made into a larger bed. Curtains here are Bennison fabrics in muted colors that are especially harmonious with the golden light and slightly hazy summer afternoons. Chinese *verre eglomise* images, an English crewelwork panel from the eighteenth century (acquired in London), and antique chests and mirrors enhance the romantic, allusive mood.

Homage to Renzo Mongiardino *Above and Opposite:* The designer has admired the romantic and theatrical interiors by cult Italian decorator/set designer Renzo Mongiardino for more than two decades. For the guest suite, a vast collection of hand-blocked Indian bedspreads from Urban Outfitters (read, very inexpensive) were matched and stitched most elegantly into handsome curtains. They were also mitered and artfully attached to the walls and ceiling, complete with borders, to give the impression of an Anglo-Indian tent in Rajasthan—or Sintra, or Venice. Mongiardino, memorably, tented rooms in the Palazzo Brandolini on Venice's Grand Canal, in similar hand-blocked Indian fabrics in these same traditional madder-dyed fabrics. A series of watercolors depicting traditional Turkish costumes animate the walls.

THE ART OF THE CALIFORNIA HACIENDA

It is a classic hacienda, a hilltop ranch house attributed to Cliff May, and like most Los Angeles houses, it comes with a movie-star pedigree. This handsome residence in Brentwood is reputed to have been the home of Academy Award–winning actor, Ronald Coleman in the thirties and forties. It is now the family home of film and television producer, Brian Grazer, and his wife, Gigi Levangie Grazer, an author and screenwriter.

The house commands a rustic canyon with ocean views beyond, and offers the peace and privacy the owners craved. "The Grazers called me two years ago because they no longer found the décor appropriate and they wanted a fresh, more personal look," said Michael Smith. "We redesigned every part of the interiors, every surface, each beam, every mantel, each color. There was not a lamp we could salvage from the previous décor. We went in a totally new direction."

Smith's concept was to restore the integrity of its original architecture, to open rooms, lighten the décor, and make it a fine setting for the Grazers' considerable art collection, which includes pieces by Gerhard Richter, Andy Warhol, Richard Prince, and iconic paintings of the late twentieth century.

Family Time *Above:* For the Grazer family house, Michael Smith and his clients chose iconic mid-century modern furniture with a cool vibe. The plan was to choose furniture and accessories with great individuality, but to bring them together in a way that is family-friendly, not museum-like. *Opposite:* In a corner of the family room, which is adjacent to the kitchen, an Ed Ruscha painting hangs above a new stone fireplace surround. Michael Smith combined vintage twentieth-century designs with a Japanese lacquered table.

"We wanted to keep the rooms simple and authentic, so we used natural Belgian linen and burlap curtains," says the designer. Walls were finished with elegant oyster-colored, textured Venetian plaster as a foil for the large canvases. It is all very discreet.

"It's such a misconception that people who are successful in the entertainment industry want glitzy and glamorous houses," says Smith. "The great myth is that they want mirrors or Mylar so that they can glimpse their reflections coming and going. Nothing could be further from the truth. The reality is that people in the whirlwind of movies and music are interested in quality, lasting values, not mere glitter. My clients have a much more evolved and sophisticated approach. They're immersed in today's culture, and approach design with a practiced eye. They realize the value of ideas, of a lively collaboration, of acquiring objects with a rich history."

It would have been predictable to paint the walls white to show off the large paintings. "Hard white is too stark in this setting, and unrelieved white tends to make even great art look cheap," Smith says. "The art is more visually powerful on a textural background. Venetian plaster makes the paintings part of a composition that's both pleasing and balanced."

The designer intensified the richness of the plaster walls with antique carpets and textiles, and a highly specialized gathering of vintage furniture.

"I do what's right for each client, for each house, and I reinvent design for each client," says Smith. "Brian and Gigi came to this project with fantastic art. My plan was to add texture and variation to the interiors, inspired by the architecture and the location. I don't separate the practical and appropriate from the decorative and aesthetic considerations, and that approach works best for me."

The designer began with great respect for the architectural traditions of the house. "I am always about a classical approach," says Smith. "Whether the architecture is modern or traditional in nature, I have great respect for it; I bring out its best features and strengths. But I give it a twist. I don't do theme design. One-note design is not my style."

Individual Footprint *Above:* Michael Smith believes in the late interior designer Elsie de Wolfe's aesthetic of "light, air and comfort," and also in giving rooms texture, personality, and surprise. In the living room, a large coffee table with a crackled lacquer finish stands up to a bold Louis XIV–style chair with a leather-covered back and seat. The Turkish carpet and African and Indian textiles add spice, texture, and color to an otherwise neutral palette.

Gather Around *Opposite:* An eighteenth-century stone mantel, one of five antique stone mantels added to the Grazers' house, makes a soft background for a bold reproduction Spanish colonial table. "I chose the antique Spanish chairs for their sense of solidity, and for their comfort," said the designer, who acquired them at auction. The shoes painting is by Andy Warhol.

The Grazers are always looking at and acquiring new art, and are intrigued by thinkers and artists outside the entertainment industry. "Brian and Gigi are constant students of pop culture and the creative world," says Smith. "They were fantastic clients, and their open-mindedness and enthusiasm made them very interesting to work with."

The house is everyone's image of a classic rambling ranch house, and it needed to be updated with great sensitivity. "As we worked to improve the flow of the rooms and to give logic and comfort to the interiors, I was always thinking about lighting, and practical matters like art instal-lation, bookcases, and picture hanging, and the specialists we would need," says the designer.

The Grazers are involved with environmental causes, fund-raising for education, and a wide range of political issues, and the house often fills with crowds of friends and political action groups.

"The interiors are cheerful, soothing, and rich in detail—whether for one person or a group," said Smith. "Each room is layered with paintings, iconic Spanish antique furniture, books, views, tribal rugs and ethnic textiles. The eye is constantly intrigued."

Privacy and Peace *Above:* In the bathroom, hand-painted striped wallpaper by Elizabeth Dow, New York, adds a subtle texture and tone to the walls. The For Town bathtub is from the Michael Smith Collection for Kallista.

Perchance to Wake *Opposite:* An Indian four-poster made from padouk wood, and a pair of nineteenth-century Chinese tables make a graphic contrast to the paint-ing *Rorschach* (1984) by Andy Warhol. The bedroom and sitting room have beautiful light and high ceilings, which bestow a certain tranquility.

A HOUSE WITH HISTORY

In Beverly Hills, nearly every house comes with an architectural pedigree, a history, and famous former owners. In the case of Rupert and Wendi Murdoch's house, the architect was Wallace Neff, a Pasadena native who designed some of the most elegant Spanish and Mediterranean-style baronial residences in Los Angeles. Neff became known as the architect of California's golden age. The house, called Misty Mountain, was also the former residence of Jules and Doris Stein. Dr. Stein, an ophthalmologist from the Midwest, founded the giant Music Corporation of America, and later acquired Universal Pictures. His wife, Doris, was a noted hostess and style maker. The couple, kingpins of the social set, were devoted Anglophiles who collected English furniture, architectural details, and textiles.

When the Murdochs acquired their house, they also kept much of its museum-worthy furniture collection, as well as rooms with seventeenth-century English fumed oak–paneled walls.

The Murdochs wanted the house to have a calm mien. In the living room, cream wool suiting fabric softens the highly detailed interior architecture. Chairs are upholstered in woven tone-on-tone silk and linen fabrics. A pale ivory, document-inspired damask was used on the eighteenth-century English mahogany furniture.

The intent was to bring out the fine carving of the antiques and to give the living room a cohesive, polished feeling. The pale cream tones also act as a neutral canvas for the Murdochs' collection of contemporary Australian art.

An Elegant Impression *Opposite and following pages:* In Rupert and Wendi Murdoch's living room, English fumed-oak wall panels are carved with traditional strap work. By simplifying the pale ivory color scheme and adding a pale blue Tabriz carpet, the highly detailed rooms became calmer, quieter. The coffee table has a crackled-linen finish. The lamps are antique Chinese.

IN A BRENTWOOD CANYON

A few years ago, while searching for a change of pace from his oft-photographed Santa Monica sea-view penthouse, Michael Smith came upon a simple sixties Arizona adobe Modernist house hidden on a steep hillside in a Brentwood canyon. Spare but robust, it had never been remodeled, and it was a clean slate for experimentation. The first act was to clear away the brown veneer walls, then to whitewash the exposed bricks. Wall-to-wall carpet was donated to a local charity, leaving the bare hardwood floors and terra-cotta tiles exposed. A new stainless steel and cherry kitchen was installed, along with three new bathrooms. Finally, the *Brady Bunch* retro feeling was banished, and the house felt modern and refreshed, as relaxed as a sunny house in Los Angeles can possibly be.

Mix Master *Above:* White-painted textured walls in the study bring contrast and mood to a mid-century modern table, here used as a desk. *Opposite:* "I'm opposed to narrowness of taste and lazy design," Michael Smith said. The massive beams of the living room ceiling were exposed when Smith stripped the house down to its bones. The structure's International/Modernist style is tempered with organic materials like terra-cotta tiles and white-painted brick walls. Rejecting theme design, Smith selected antiques and new furniture for integrity, craftsmanship, and character.

Nothing in Smith's interiors is too formulaic or too "done." He insists that style can be found at any price level. His favored sources range from Parisian antiquaries to Target and Urban Outfitters. When designing for himself, the décor is open-ended, spare, and understated.

"For my projects, I obsess about the hand-plastered walls or the exact finish of a plank floor or a gilded frame because that's what gives me pleasure and will please my clients—perhaps merely subliminally," Smith said. "If just one of the design elements of a room is not perfect, if the interior architecture is off balance, then the room is just not going to be up to snuff. For myself, I'm more laissez-faire. But even a room that's overtly casual should have superb lighting and good art."

Breakfast with Style *Above and Opposite:* The dining area looks onto the entry courtyard, with its olive trees, river stones, and a small reflecting pool. The vintage table is by Jean Prouvé.

The house, since sold, offered large, high-ceilinged rooms and a splendid bathroom overlooking an enclosed courtyard, very L.A. "The ultimate luxury in Los Angeles today is not a gold-plated bathroom or fur throws or hand-woven silk draperies with hand-beaded tassels," said the designer. "We all work hard. What everyone, including myself, really needs is a good night's sleep and a beautifully appointed bathroom with all the bells and whistles. I turn on the bath, light candles, make a quiet ritual out of a late-night soak. And I need a beautiful bedroom, the right custom-made mattress, the perfect lighting for reading in bed, and a place for complete, blissful rest."

Confident Contrasts *Above and Opposite:* Michael Smith insists on natural materials and low-key colors that are at one with the surroundings. He remodeled his three bathrooms with Ann Sacks glass tiles, a Kohler whirlpool, simple glass windows, and a limestone steam shower. It is peaceful here, although coyotes often howl in the canyon beyond the terrace. Pure white linens in the bedroom are by Calvin Klein Home. The dramatically colored bedcover is an antique *suzani*, hand-embroidered and appliquéd.

A HAPPY HOUSE IN BEL-AIR

It could have seemed unlikely that superhot fashion designer Mossimo Giannulli and his equally trend-savvy wife, actress Lori Loughlin, would fall in love with a twenties manor house in Bel-Air attributed to architect Gordon Kauffman. The house, complete with a turret, had once been glamorous, but its former grandeur had been obliterated with mirrored walls, track lighting, and other misguided attempts at modernization. "It was all very Zsa Zsa Gabor," recalled Loughlin.

Giannulli is the design genius that turns offbeat,

iconoclastic, and hip fashion into gold for Target. Loughlin is the blonde whose sweet and droll delivery was perfected on the television shows *Full House* and *Summerland.*

The couple saw through the mess to the house's possibilities. They engaged Michael Smith and his frequent design collaborator, Oscar Shamanian, to return the house to its former glory. In spite of the fact that they have two young children, the couple defied expectations by seeking out serious antiques, paled-down colors, and bolts of luscious silk fabrics.

Young Couple, Elegant House *Above, Opposite, and Following Pages:* Lori Loughlin loved the romance of two-tone silk curtains with all the glamour of a vintage ball gown. The Kopla silk is by the Silk Trading Co. The living room was restored and reimagined, with new moldings and a new fireplace, antique Chinese lacquered tables, a George III chair, and richly ornamented carpets that are truly family-friendly. "This interior was all about mixing greens and blues and giving the room an elegance that was lighthearted, a bit flip, and very youthful, not too serious," said Michael Smith. The subtext here is a reductive version of a traditional sitting room (the house required a nod to the traditional) but with contemporary photography, abstract paintings, and lots of air and light as a counterpoint.

Smith worked with Giannulli and Loughlin to recreate their house, focusing on enriching the interiors with the detail and clarity the space lacked, but refraining from creating a pastiche. "You have to be careful when restoring old houses that you don't go too far with mood creation and end up with an unfortunate, over-the-top bad Merchant Ivory look," said Smith. "It's best to hold back a bit, so that the houses look modern and youthful, not heavy-handed."

All three tracked down and selected the antiques that would be both formal and whimsical. Coral-pink leather dresses up a George III chair, and windows are romanced with vivid blue and green silk curtains with silvery tiebacks.

This Just In *Above and Opposite:* First order of business in the project was to renovate the kitchen, family room, and dining room, which are connected by elegant, tall archways. Mossimo Giannulli wanted surprises, a dash of both the unexpected and subversive, so they installed an antique wood-and-glass Chinese lantern, nickel hardware, and lighting and furniture that had a period feeling without being overly heavy on the theatrics. Colors—both bright and subdued—channel David Hicks, who knew a thing or two about freshening up grand and traditional houses in the sixties. But it is the personal collections that bring it all alive. Throughout the house the couple has hung favorite pieces from their photography collection, including a series of William Claxton's portraits, Sid Avery's Rat Pack images, and Slim Aarons's revered portraits of C.Z. Guest. There are framed images from classic children's books, and walls hung with skateboards and surfboards—as well as Giannulli's music memorabilia and classic motorcycles. Now the house truly fits the couple.

Scrolls and Curves *Opposite and Above:* The Giannulli family are generous and thoughtful hosts. For this guest room, Smith designed walls with pressed birchboard panels to give a shimmering, textural look. The curtains of Chinese wild silk (untreated raw silk) were crafted simply and now hang over vermicelli-thin bamboo blinds for subtle light control and privacy. A series of architectural drawings were found in New York, London, and Paris, and the Scottish hall chair with a bull's-eye back was a London find.

A GENEROUS SPIRIT

Writer/director/actor/producer Rob Reiner and his wife, photographer Michele Singer Reiner, were among Michael Smith's first clients when he founded his design firm in 1992. They have all become close friends, so Smith is often invited to their house in Brentwood for birthday parties, family dinners, and frequent fund-raisers for the Reiners' favorite political issues. Among the guests are likely to be politicians, movie stars, and other major talents, both on-screen and off.

"The Reiners' house is like an open-hearted club-house for Saturday night screenings, philanthropic events, and celebrations for their three children," said Smith. "It's Connecticut-meets-Colonial, a *Bringing Up Baby* kind of house, and it is very much a family home."

It is the kind of house the designer loves to work on,

with motivated clients and collections that will add personality to the décor.

"Michele has a significant collection of black-and-white photography, as well as turn-of-the-century California plein air paintings," said Smith. "She's also a very talented and serious photographer, so we saw the house in muted, black-and-white terms. There's not a lot of color."

For the décor, which is sculptural in feeling, Smith channeled Frances Elkins, the trendsetting California decorator who in the thirties introduced both Jean-Michel Frank and Alberto Giacometti to the United States.

"Michele has a great editorial eye, and she adheres to the discipline of black and white both in interiors and in her own fashion," said Smith. "She wears mostly black."

Rose Is a Rose Is a Rose *Above and Opposite:* Rob Reiner and Michele Singer Reiner's house in Brentwood is surrounded by well-established grounds upon which Michele has lavished her love and attention. Roses bloom around the screening room, which is located in a separate building adjacent to the Colonial-style house. Michael Smith redesigned the entry hall and added a grand antique table. The décor preserves the forties quality of the house, but is somewhat spare.

One of the reasons the Reiners' family house is so comfortable, so warm-hearted, is that it is completely private, hidden behind gardens and trees in a leafy corner of Brentwood, far from the high-profile Beverly Hills–Bel-Air axis. Life in Brentwood, which is situated between Bel-Air and Santa Monica, is more relaxed, quieter, and less formal.

"The Reiners' house feels like it's in a very elegant part of Connecticut, or even Cape Cod," said Smith. "They love their home, and use it well and generously. They're always opening it for their friends' causes, and for parties for their children's friends. Whenever I'm there, I'm likely to find kids' games and wonderful entertainment."

To make the house at once stylish and elegant yet practical, Smith stained all the floors dark mahogany. "It took weeks and many coats of stain to get it right and to get the density we wanted," recalled the designer. Walls were painted a pale oyster white, which takes on a golden glow in the afternoon.

Adjacent to the house is a screening room, one of many Michael Smith has designed for his clients, many of whom are involved in the entertainment industry.

Photo Inspiration *Opposite and Right:* The living room is mostly off-white, with ivory upholstery and washable slipcovers. Floors are stained deep mahogany, and furniture is sculptural rather than fussy. Accessories, such as stoneware pitchers and pillows, are kept within the neutral color palette.

Welcome, Friends *Left and Above:* The dark stained floors lend a strong foundation to the décor and add continuity from room to room. Smith arranged a series of fine Oriental rugs that are not so precious that spilled juice or wine would worry the hostess. French painted chairs are arranged around an Italian walnut neoclassical table.

Transformation and Custom Crafting *Above and Right:* The Reiners' bedroom and spacious bathroom were carved from a former study/office. The wood floor was painted to resemble a traditional marble floor—but with a light touch, no verisimilitude intended. Doors lead to a secluded garden. It is a his-and-hers bathroom, the ideal kind, with lots of light and large mirrors, and—as an unexpected touch—an antique pedestal table and chairs.

Bathing Beauty *Above:* In the screening room bath, Smith installed a handpainted floor, and an antique pedestal sink and tub discovered in Maine.

The Pleasure of Your Company *Right:* Private screening rooms are ubiquitous in Los Angeles and most of Smith's clients have one. The surprise is that while they are superbly equipped with the latest in technology, most of them are very traditional in style, with well-stuffed armchairs, Oriental carpets, chandeliers, and a crystal bowl of candy. Smith and the Reiners renovated this formerly very seventies screening room, opening up the ceiling to expose the beams. (The previous owner was Norman Lear.)

A FAMILY HOUSE IN BRENTWOOD PARK

Gary Gersh and Maria Mancuso Gersh are both well-referenced aficionados of Los Angeles architecture, so it is not surprising that they chose for themselves a neo-Georgian house by the celebrated Paul R. Williams, the first African-American member and fellow of the American Institute of Architects.

Williams, who designed more than three thousand projects during his fifty-year career, specialized in houses that were opulent, spacious, a little bit Hollywood, and always very welcoming. His clients included Tyrone Power, Frank Sinatra, and Barbara Stanwyck.

The Gershes admired the structure's fluted columns, arched doorways, highly theatrical hallways, and oval windows. Working with Michael Smith, and architects Tichenor and Thorp, they wanted to return the house to its original glamour. Balancing luxury and practicality, they rethought the big entrance hall, removed a fake fireplace, freshened the living room, redesigned the kitchen, and turned "this radiant environment," as Williams called it, into a wonderful family home.

Cinema Verité *Above and Opposite:* Classicist architect Paul R. Williams designed the Gershes' house in the early twentieth-century for comedienne ZaSu Pitts. It is a cinematic version of an English cottage, in grand style, created in white-painted brick. A framed Amish striped quilt hangs above an eighteenth-century English sofa on the upstairs landing. The walls are covered in handmade Swedish wallpaper.

The Gershes' house, surrounded by a lush garden, was built in 1936 for actress ZaSu Pitts. It was romantic and picturesque in its parklike setting, but it also needed a complete makeover. Previous owners had tinkered with its fine lines, and thanks to a noted entertainer who doted on Victoriana, ornate moldings and carved cupids lurked in many rooms. In Williams's original plans, which the Gershes consulted, there was a secret staircase that led up to the actress's boudoir. It was a playful, cinematic gesture, typical of the sweeping and personal vision for the interior architecture.

Working closely with the Gershes, Smith found important antiques, many of them with bold, sculptural lines. For the hall, there was a forties French table with a beveled top and curved pedestal base. A mahogany Regency cabinet decorated with a star and arrow motif was another lucky find. There was also a new Anglo-Indian-style dining table, and cane-seated Anglo-Indian chairs to add a certain exoticism.

One very fortunate auction discovery was early thirties Zuber wallpaper depicting a muted El Dorado landscape with plumed peacocks and full-blown roses in a pattern dating back to the early nineteenth century. It now covers one wall in the garden room, giving the house a ravishing sense of the dreamy past.

Gracious Welcome *Above:* The art of greeting guests is enhanced by the handsome center table and pair of versatile stools, which can be pressed into service as instant, elegant seating when guests spill in from a cocktail gathering or dinner. *Opposite:* In the garden room, a theatrical Zuber wallpaper creates a leafy and exotic stage set that is visible from the front entry hall.

The Strength of Repetition *Left and Above:* The dining room is romantic yet family-friendly. The custom-crafted dining table was inspired by an Anglo-Indian original (which was too small). The original Paul Williams architectural detail is intact and the walls are painted a dreamy tone of ice blue, the perfect contrast to the dark silhouettes of the chair backs.

Maria Gersh, a designer and photography collector, wanted the bedroom suite to be a bit whimsical—lighthearted and youthful. Smith worked on a pale white-and-cream color scheme with curtains of sheer Irish handkerchief linen, and walls painted a lavender-tinted white.

Maria commented to Michael that she wanted her bedroom to look like an out-of-focus black-and-white photograph. He captured her dream with a grand Venetian mirror, paired with a Venetian four-poster bed with a curved headboard draped lavishly with blue-and-white striped silk.

And there is the tour de force of the residence, an oval-shaped loggia that opens to the sheltered garden. It is furnished for either casual entertaining or quiet relaxation with a pair of thirties metal garden chairs, and a curved sofa covered in the palest turquoise canvas, and pillows of La Rose chintz by Brunschwig & Fils.

Mirror/Mirror *Above and Opposite*: The bed, lavished with heirloom French and Italian embroidered linens, is reflected in an antique Venetian mirror. A William IV mahogany desk from Niall Smith in New York stands in the sunny bay window of the bedroom. Creamy silken linen curtains give the room a sumptuous but relaxed look.

BESIDE THE SEA

It is just twenty minutes from Beverly Hills to Malibu along winding Sunset Boulevard, but the ocean setting is another world of fresh sea air, quiet, and a feeling of being incredibly fortunate, permanently on vacation. It is there overlooking the Pacific Ocean that Donna Arkoff Roth, a film producer, owns a house in the Malibu Colony. Her family retreat, built in the thirties, is a timber-and-stucco mock-Tudor structure surrounded by a lush garden. The fragrance of honeysuckle and jasmine lingers in the air. It is a handsome house, with a somewhat eccentric, off-kilter floor plan that enhances the mood of relaxation and ease. Far from slick, the house has quirky Dutch doors with leaded-glass windows, an enclosed beachside terrace, and lots of fireplaces to ward off Malibu's nighttime chill. The big surprise in fabled and golden endless-summer Malibu is that winters can be cool, and that summer mornings may be foggy. But there is always direct access to the beach, which makes this one of the most coveted spots in all of Los Angeles.

Layers of Comfort *Above and Opposite:* Rather than an all-white beach house look, the 20-by-40-foot living room is layered in easygoing chintzes and linen fabrics and painted furniture and antiques that look as if they have inhabited the room for decades. In fact, they are all new to the house. The casual vibe of the beach house is enhanced by its open floor plan, and the large new doorways that give a feeling of fresh air, ease, and flexibility. A collection of nautical paintings honors the seaside setting, while the fresh and friendly décor intentionally steps back from playing to a beach theme.

Donna Roth's beach house, with its reclaimed chestnut floors, Maine wicker sofas, collections of Welsh creamware, and blue-and-white checked linens, is more formal New England in style than it is surfer cool in the cinematic image of beach party Malibu of *How to Stuff a Wild Bikini* fame. (Roth's father, producer Samuel Z. Arkoff, produced beach-blanket and teen monster flicks.) The thirties house had been remodeled over the decades, and had been overlaid with faux glamour, so the plan was to install antique fireplaces, add appropriate architectural detailing, and return a solid feeling of tradition and classicism. The newly shaped architecture was guided by New York architect Oscar Shamamian. Most of all, the concept was to make it a year-round refuge, a place where kids in wet swimsuits and friends with sand on their feet could relax in the sunroom or read beside the fire.

A Sense of Freedom *Left:* Donna Roth's Malibu house was designed to welcome friends and keep the mood light, relaxed, and calm. The interiors are understated, with antiques and carpets that are barefoot-friendly and have soft signs of age and time. Sand and sun can only make them more appealing and pleasing. Walls are painted a soft, rich cream tone, edged with white. The red eighteenth-century chest of drawers greets guests in the entrance hall, newly remodeled by architect Oscar Shamamian.

To the Horizon *Following pages:* The upstairs bedroom, with its exposed beams and creamy yellow and pale blue palette, has a sitting area occupied by a capacious sofa covered in a beloved English chintz and doors leading to a terrace overlooking the beach. To liven things up, Michael Smith added an antique Agra carpet, a faux-bamboo bed, and a collection of Imperial Yellow Peking glass that glows in the afternoon sun.

IN THE CLOUDS

From the legendary towers of The Carlyle in New York, apartment windows afford unimpeded views across the trees and meadows of Central Park to the misty Hudson River and beyond. Madison Avenue is far below, its speeding taxis blissfully out of earshot.

It was exactly this discreet, beautifully poised setting that appealed to the new owners, who live for most of the year in California but wanted a chic pied-à-terre in Manhattan. There, minutes from the Bemelmans Bar, the Café Carlyle, Fifth Avenue, and Park Avenue, they enjoy a light-filled apartment of surpassing beauty.

These longtime clients of Smith wanted a retreat from the hustle and bustle, a pale and ethereal aerie with a sense of architecture, a feeling of expansiveness.

Oscar Shamamian, of Ferguson & Shamamian, planned a new, lighthearted interior architecture. He stripped the rooms down to the radiator caps, but did not move walls. New bleached-oak parquetry replaced dark flooring. Tall mahogany doors were installed to add a sense of luxury and to give a feeling of height to the principal rooms. He added new classical cornices, elegantly proportioned baseboards, and sterling silver hardware to add visual complexity and to restore a sense of glamorous thirties New York.

Textural Contrasts *Above:* The worlds of art and nature come together superbly and surprisingly with a Gandhara Buddha head and a shell, which rests on a nineteenth-century French gilt stand. In pleasing juxtaposition, a Winslow Homer pen-and-ink hangs above a Georgian gilt table. The random markings on the marble top seem to mirror Homer's deft brushstrokes. The English table is topped with a seventeenth-century Persian urn.

A Sense of Formality *Opposite:* In the entrance hall and living room, pale parquetry floors, in a large-scale pattern, bring a sense of drama and modernism. A demi-lune table was selected for its graceful silhouette. The torso is Roman. A pair of marble columns topped with stone urns flank the mahogany doors.

High Above Central Park *Following Pages:* From the living room windows, framed with simple cream-colored curtains, it is possible to see across the billowing green treetops of the park to the romantic turrets along Central Park West. The secretary, balanced with a pair of gilt sconces, gives a sense of architecture and stature to the room. The painted ivory chairs are from H.M. Luther Antiques, New York City. The interior architecture, which was stripped and redesigned to make it expansive and visually balanced, is by Oscar Shamamian of New York-based Ferguson & Shamamian.

The décor of this pied-à-terre has a sense of stateliness and tradition, but with a more eccentric and modern approach, not an attempt to create the look of an ancestral home. While the apartment is large and sweeping, and the antiques exude a sense of quality and superb craftsmanship, the overall effect is light, fresh, and exquisitely understated.

The apartment occupies more than two-thirds of a floor high in the Carlyle tower. One task was to give it a feeling of a private residence, rather than a hotel suite occasionally occupied. To this end, each painting and each piece of furniture was hand-selected for its character, its intrinsic beauty, and for its ineffable charm. There is practicality to the design, too. Tables and chairs are multipurpose. A circa 1820 Cuban mahogany dining table can also perform smoothly as a book table. A sculptural series of Russian neoclassical mahogany chairs ornamented with parcel-gilt and ormolu work perfectly as dining chairs, and swing into action as occasional chairs when guests arrive.

Lap of Luxury *Opposite:* A Georgian roll-top desk and a Jackie O coffee table from Erica Brunson add texture to this corner of the living room thirty stories high. The painted and silver-gilt table is from Madeleine Castaing. *Above:* A neoclassical French center table with brass trim and a trio of Russian chairs from the Romanov family collection can be used for dining, reading, or a luxurious breakfast. The painting is by Henri-Pierre Danloux.

Sweet Rest *Opposite and Above:* In the bedroom, a polished brass and steel canopy bed topped with gilt finials, gives a sense of repose in a room within a room. A Pierre-Jacques Volaire painting of a volcano illuminates the corner. On an early-nineteenth-century Russian commode stand a series of Chinese teardrop and double-gourd vases and urns, and a Franz Kline watercolor.

A Tracery of Leaves *Following pages:* A wallcovering depicting vines, leaves, and flowers brings a feeling of escapism to the guest bedroom. The patterned paper also disguises the slight awkwardness of the space. A circa 1825 Italian neoclassical bed with gilt finials and fine marquetry animates the room and adds detail and importance to the small room. The elaborate bed is balanced with a simple alabaster lamp base, unadorned wool twill curtains, and a gilt mirror with a rather understated frame.

A TASTE FOR GLAMOUR

Michael Smith has designed five homes for Cindy Crawford, and they have become close friends. When the supermodel, whose glorious face has graced more than five hundred international magazine covers, acquired a sunny apartment on the Upper East Side in Manhattan, it was natural that she and her husband, Rande Gerber, would rely on the designer to give it balance, exuberance, and a touch of exoticism.

The three-bedroom apartment, in a thirties building on Madison Avenue, had ten-foot ceilings, well-proportioned rooms, and great potential. Working with architect Oscar Shamamian, Smith reshaped the rooms to give the layout bet-

ter flow, and to afford a more practical use of space.

The furniture is dramatic and lush, with large tufted ottomans accompanying leather sofas, and a green-and-white-checked wing chair from Amy Perlin Antiques curving beside a pair of English club-style slipcovered armchairs. The mood is traditional yet youthful.

The eighteenth-century English mahogany table in the entry foyer has a thick Egyptian-alabaster top. Continuing the cosmopolitan collection, the couple's four-poster bed is Anglo-Indian in style, a Venetian mirror sparkles in the bedroom, an Agra carpet soothes the living room, while an elaborately carved table in the living room is from Morocco.

No Place Like Home *Above*: In the entrance of Cindy Crawford's Manhattan apartment, the floors are English limestone, and the walls are Venetian plaster.. *Opposite*: Model/actress/spokesperson/fund-raiser Cindy Crawford, a longtime Michael Smith client, wanted a "homey," comfortable, and practical décor for her family's apartment in Manhattan. In the study, natural cotton canvas was painted by artist Jim Russell to give the effect of antique leather, and applied to the walls. An antique Dutch mirror and large-scale furniture give the small room a feeling of comfort and stature. Photographs by San Francisco photographers Ruth Bernhard and Imogen Cunningham bring the room into the twentieth century. The antique Chinese low table is from ABC Carpet and Home. *Following pages*: Michael Smith worked with New York–based architect Oscar Shamamian to update and reshape architectural details of the apartment. The architect designed the new stone mantelpiece in the living room. The wing chair was originally used in Crawford's previous New York apartment. The Agra carpet is from Y & B Bolour.

East Side Living *Opposite and Above:* Smith has collaborated with Crawford on several houses and apartments on both coasts, and they work on her interiors using a combination of shorthand, mental telepathy, and good humor. "Cindy is confident of her taste and prefers large-scale furniture that is truly comfortable and has a timeless style," said the designer. "She's been collecting black-and-white photography for years, and these pieces work well with paintings, antiques and great old rugs we've found together. She's not a fan of itsy-bitsy things, and prefers solid, functional pieces in wood, leather and bronze. But we keep it light, family-friendly, easy to maintain, and welcoming." In the dining room and living room, a large scroll-arm sofa, a Regency-style dining table, a billiard-table light fixture, substantial chairs, and a wing chair covered in a Brunschwig & Fils checked fabric show the designer's deft arrangements and choices.

Pale Romance *Left and Opposite:* The bedroom was designed to be a calm, uncluttered refuge from the noise and intensity of the city outside. The four-poster, inspired by an Anglo-Indian original, and a mother-of-pearl inlaid chest bring an air of exoticism. Antique Venetian mirrors, a Whartonian portrait in a gilt frame, simple cream bed linens, and an antique bamboo chair add to the graceful, understated mood.

ROMANCE AND RIGOR IN BEVERLY HILLS

Beverly Hills is one of the most coveted addresses in the world, and not merely for its Hollywood connections. With its leafy estates, winding jacaranda-shaded avenues, privileged hillside perches, and a feeling of permanent springtime, Beverly Hills provides a setting both for glamorous lives and quiet retreats.

Roger and Pamela Birnbaum found their 10,000-square-foot house there. But like the best Hollywood stories, they had to create the happy ending. On first sight the residence was over-the-top eighties glitz, with acres of black granite, bleached floors, and steel fireplaces. But there was a columned loggia and a pretty garden, the scale was gener-

ous, ceilings were high, and the house had an impressive entrance hall with a retractable glass ceiling—simply press a button and it opens to the sky.

Michael Smith's first take and inspiration on décor is often an iconic film. In this case it was *Boom*, a sixties camp classic starring Elizabeth Taylor, who swept around an Italian Modernist house on craggy Sardinia. With thoughts of forties Italian glamour and an Art Deco villa in Rome dancing in his head, he and the Birnbaums went for rigor with romance, respecting the reality of the architecture while giving the rooms a modern, warm feeling of aesthetic humanism.

Noble Columns *Above:* Exuberant bougainvillea and citrus trees give an Amalfi Coast mood to the loggia, which is furnished with chairs and tables from Janus et Cie.

Family Values *Opposite:* Michael Smith gave the living room some impressive decorating muscle with a French forties-style sofa (upholstered in chocolate velvet from Nancy Corzine) and chaise (covered in Shan silk from Larsen) and a massive antique Dutch mirror. The cocktail table was crafted by the Atelier Viollet to look like an African-inspired forties design by Jean-Michel Frank.

The Birnbaums appreciated the large windows and the heroic scale of doorways and halls, but the house required serious editing and a careful redirection of the interior. Out went the bleached floors, to be replaced with cherry in a classic, practical herringbone pattern. Banished was the steel, along with everything flashy and hard-edged. When materials could be saved, they were restyled. One black granite fireplace in the living room was toned down by honing the stone to a friendly matte finish.

There was also the matter of light. While the house was blessed with the overscale windows and large doors, it was also shaded with a canopy of mature trees and framed by tall walls to protect privacy. Smith solved the light problem by keeping walls pale and creamy and dressing the windows with ultrasimple, cream-colored wool curtains by Rogers & Goffigon, lined and back-lit with yellow wool. The effect is ethereal and very success-ful, and there always seems to be sunshine filtering in through the windows. It is a theatrical design trick, and it works, especially in winter.

Distinctive Style *Above and Opposite:* The dining room is animated by a collection of colorful Venetian glass collections and a table designed by Michael Smith. Above a forties Italian cabinet from Amy Perlin Antiques in New York, a 1927 Vittorio Zecchini Murano chandelier is reflected in a mirrored niche. In the breakfast room, a new beech fireplace surround gives the space a warmth it lacked in its previous eighties glitz-and-glamour years.

Sumptuous Splendor *Above and Opposite:* The bedroom suite includes an office/study, which is furnished with a Mattaliano sofa covered in a Clarence House cotton/linen fabric. Its Chinese-style wallpaper, a romantic depiction of sinuous branches and swooping birds, recalls the Paris boudoir of Pauline de Rothschild. In the suave bedroom, bleached mahogany furniture designed by Michael Smith gives a lighthearted air. Hanging above the bed, which is dressed in Anichini linens, is a circa 1865 Japanese screen. The eighteenth-century Italian chair is from Therien & Co., Los Angeles.

CITY LIGHTS

The luxury high-rise Museum Tower was built on West 53rd Street in the eighties when The Museum of Modern Art sold its air rights. If the attraction of visiting the museum's Monets, Cézannes, and Pollocks while on the way to an appointment were not enough, the building came with versatile floor plans, high ceilings, and alluring views up and down the length of Manhattan.

Michael Smith loved the glamour of his fiftieth floor aerie, and saw the design project as a rather cinematic one. His concept was to capture the international ideal of a New York apartment in the movies, with references to seventies glamour exemplified by Halston in the Olympic Tower, James Bond movies (the Roger Moore period), Andy Warhol in Paris, Yves Saint Laurent, and interior designer François Catroux.

Here in his New York retreat was the best of all worlds: a twelve-panel Coromandel screen, a bed inspired by André Arbus, an armchair by André Sornay, a Chinese root table, and a luxe collection of silken nineteenth-century Tabriz and Turkistan carpets. It is a sensual refuge in the clouds. The Monets can wait.

Gourmet Fare *Above and Opposite:* The dining room is enlivened with the spirited oil painting, *The Tiger Hunt,* from the school of Peter Paul Rubens.

International Intrigue *Following Pages:* A twelve-panel Coromandel screen soars behind the Ming-inspired bed and gives the room a sense of height and scale. The bed is draped with an antique Turkish *suzani* fabric, a particular favorite of the designer's.

A Sleek Artifice *Pages 111–112:* Michael Smith layered textures and soft tones in his living room, and selected furniture that was chic and sculptural. The walls are covered in squares of pressed-birch paper. The pair of sofas is upholstered in linen and silk in a color described by Smith as "burnt Vermeer red." The French cabinet, right, is from Amy Perlin Antiques.

A PRIVATE HOUSE

Supermodel Cindy Crawford has been the subject of countless editorial pages over the last two decades of her career. So perhaps it is not surprising that when she went looking for a house for herself, her husband, Rande Gerber, and their two young children, she would seek out one that is completely private and hidden from view behind stately gates on a winding drive overlooking a canyon far from the dazzle of Hollywood.

The Crawford/Gerber refuge is a twenties hacienda with a gracious courtyard, surrounded by a large mature garden with a swimming pool, olive grove, fountains, and outdoor dining terraces. Most of the rooms open to the gardens, which are in bloom year-round.

There is magic in the house, too. It started life as a rather mundane ranch-style bungalow. Now the 4,000-square-foot residence looks more like the famed Hotel Bel-Air, with Spanish Colonial architecture, archways, large windows, and a sensibility that is at once gracious and relaxed.

House of Play *Above and Opposite:* Cindy Crawford loved the idea of an interior that was at once functional and romantic. Rande Gerber added his request for a theatrical spin to the décor. The living room accommodates all of their dreams with large-scale sofas covered in Bennison's India Flowers printed cotton, vintage leather chairs, and full but understated curtains crafted of Pandora linen by Rogers & Goffigon. On the mantel, a tramp art mirror and Venetian glass from J.F. Chen Antiques in Los Angeles invite a closer look.

Michael Smith has known Cindy Crawford for most of his career. They have worked on multiple projects together from Malibu to Manhattan, so they are often planning décor long distance, and the two friends speak in a kind of decorating shorthand they have perfected over the years. Smith knows that for all of Crawford's polish, she is practical and down-to-earth when it comes to her family's home. Children will be children and the décor cannot be so precious that she has to fret about trucks and paint and skateboards.

A Feeling of Ease *Left and Opposite:* One way Michael Smith made the house child-friendly was to leave lots of space around the furniture. He and Crawford selected handcrafted antique furniture in the Spanish Colonial style, which by nature is not delicate or sharp-edged. In the guest bedroom and in the principal bedroom, children can roughhouse on the antique carpets, nap or play on the beds, and read in the tufted chairs. The ebony-and-brass bed is from Michael Hollis Fine Art and Antiques. The turned-leg Villa console and carved Italian-style bed were designed by Michael Smith.

What's Cooking *Above and Opposite:* Cindy Crawford is a terrific, inventive cook, says Smith. The new kitchen was designed by architect Michael Kovac, as was the outdoor fireplace. Life here is spent outdoors much of the year, so the dining terrace is an essential addition to the house. The oversized, scalloped umbrella is by Santa Barbara Designs. The landscape design is by Christine London, Beverly Hills.

Michael S. Smith
Inspiration and Ideas

Michael Smith works for some of the most illustrious names and families on both coasts, but he is above all a practical dreamer. He is generous with his ideas, his inspirations, his design tips. "One of my favorite quick, inexpensive fixes is either to lighten or darken walls with paint," he said.

"Choosing a paint color that's a little bit unexpected will instantly change the mood and feeling of a room." He is passionate about design and always opinionated. For example, he loves a touch of eccentricity in design, adores rooms that welcome kids and dogs, and encourages his clients and anyone embarking on a design adventure to think big, to look beyond existing ideas, and to tailor rooms to dreams and fervent passions rather than existing design concepts.

Michael is open-minded about antiques, color, architecture, floors, textiles, and furniture, but he tends to dislike obvious design solutions and predictable color combinations, would have nightmares sleeping in synthetic-fiber sheets, gets a headache in cookie-cutter rooms, laughs at theme design, and never hangs paintings on hospital-white walls.

"I recently used a verdigris hand-blocked wallpaper with a stone pattern as background for a collection of modern paintings," he offered. "It looks less stark than a white wall. It's more like a museum presentation, the way the Louvre or the Uffizzi museums have always shown their collections. I like more of a sense of richness, of layering, of a suggestion of architecture that comes from a textured wall with plaster or handcrafted papers or raffia or grass-cloth. The art may be monumental, and the artifacts and antiques might be desired by museums, but it takes a lot of stunning architecture to make plain white paint sufficient."

Cozy and Traditional *Opposite:* Further proof that top Hollywood executives prefer richly detailed rooms that feel like home, rather than high-gloss, glitzy interiors. This all-new dining room feels as if it has been in the family for decades, thanks to the rich cream/butter color of the walls, the antique table, chairs and bench, and a collection of books. The rich color of the paint creates a golden glow, especially at night.

THE PROCESS OF DESIGN
Views from an Insider

Some designers have a "signature" style. They feel comfortable working in a way they've polished and perfected. My goal has always been individuality; I'm intrigued by idiosyncrasy, not formula. Whether I'm working on a country house or a city apartment, a beach retreat or a hillside mansion, I want each place to have the owner's imprint; a home should fit its residents like a glove. Each interior should only exist in that envelope, for that person, and in that location. For every client, the design is custom-colored and custom-crafted; there is no "design by the numbers" plan that can be applied from one house to another. Everyone's goal, whether you're working on your own or with a decorator, should be personal expression.

My work is often described as "approachable" and "under-done." While a room may contain a collection of Picassos or a series of paintings by Delacroix, I don't make the interior museum-like or intimidating. I've designed rooms that I consider both elegant and theatrical, but they're never overly opulent. The décor is highly detailed but not overwhelming. Nor do I overstyle rooms and cram every tabletop with bibelots and trinkets. That's just not modern.

I encourage my clients to be comfortable with a sense of luxury that's a bit pared down, and grace that comes from beautiful fabrics and rare antiques that are somewhat understated, not high-key. I love romantic rooms, but I'm also not afraid of simplicity.

I could never take California out of the way I see the world, so I prefer rooms that are more light-filled, open-ended, and improvisational. I grew up in Laguna Beach, with its misty coastal light, eucalyptus trees, and intense afternoon sunshine. Colors like moss green, sand, and taupe feel harmonious and familiar to me. California is not weighted down with design history, so I like interior decoration that is fresh and relaxed, not stiff or intimidating. I mix Japanese antiques with French forties furniture, and quirky flea market lamps with mid-century Danish glass collections.

Los Angeles has great weather all year, so in Southern California I favor light curtains; rooms that welcome dogs, kids with surfboards, and friends in wet swimsuits; and rooms that open to terraces for outdoor dining.

I would not describe myself as a hard-core modernist. Still, unless a client really loved the idea, I probably would not introduce ruffles and flourishes, or elaborate trims and bows to a room. These clutter the effect, look dated, and in the end are simply hard to take care of. (There are ways, other than piling on decoration, to make rooms memorable and fascinating.) Nor would I crowd a room with too many chairs and ottomans and table legs; these obscure other things that I might prefer to see, like antique carpets or a pair of exquisite French andirons.

People are complex; interiors need to reflect that complexity. I always work with a concept, and blueprint and clear plans for each interior, and with the big picture of the house in mind. However, I like to leave some space for improvisation or input from the client, like a move in a different direction or a new idea.

There also has to be room for change in a house over time. When the décor is locked in from the start, the result often looks too formal, too "done," too set in its ways. Rooms have to have life, vitality, and the glimmer of ease; otherwise they quickly look boring. Unlike many designers, I like to build in a certain under-decoration to allow for flexibility, for new uses and developments over the years, or for new additions to the rooms or to the house.

For example, in an informal dining room used every day, I'll include furnishings that can easily become elegant for a special celebration or once the children are grown. This "growing" décor does not have to be completely reinvented for its new purpose—simply restyled and refreshed.

A GOOD START

A small budget should not deter you. I love to work with younger clients in their starter bungalow or apartment. They may not have a large budget, but we begin a plan for purchases over time. Enthusiasm for the process and patience in the search for quality are more important than money.

Good architecture is a turn-on. Choose a house with good "bones" and an interesting history: these are the makings of a great home. When a structure has a wonderful provenance—noted architecture, even an architect who was once very popular but who has fallen out of favor—that can be a wonderful challenge, especially if the architecture is intact, and has not been ruined by remodeling.

Character Building *Opposite:* In film producer Donna Roth's Brentwood house, Michael Smith added a series of paintings of Vesuvius, a pottery collection, and a French Gothic-style candlestick lamp above a French provincial table with a red leather top. The quirky ensemble adds complexity and pared-down luxury to the straightforward architecture.

Design is my life. Even on weekends I'm spending time with clients, reading auction catalogs and attending sales, traveling to art shows or to antiques exhibitions, or meeting up-and-coming art dealers. The best decorators, antiques dealers, and art dealers are people who work hard and are constantly involved in their fields.

Decoration can often seem so simple. It appears that you take a striped fabric and a floral fabric and some chenille and an old rug, and you're almost there. Well, that barebones, basic approach is not decorating; it's barely furnishing. Good decoration is not about "matching," or "co-coordinating," or producing theme design—or even filling a room full of antiques or mid-century classics. Rather, it's about bringing together beautiful and practical things to create a harmonious and unique ensemble.

This surprise in décor can be dissonance. A good room will always have contrast: the juxtaposition of large- and small-scale furniture, of old and new pieces, of smooth and textured materials and surfaces.

Good design is hard work. Ultimately, you have to be happy with the effect, the way it works, and the way rooms look throughout the day and night. The design must be cohesive. That's why I would tell clients who are "shopping" for a decorator not to be swayed when a designer or contractor offers them a "deal." Good design takes time. That translates to established hourly fees and professional rates. The process is very time-consuming, and often expensive. Custom design occasionally means delivery delays, unforeseen changes, and unexpected directions.

A good designer will be a sounding board, and will evaluate each step so that there are no surprises. It's not a positive sign when a designer agrees with everything. There should be a dialogue, with some professional objectivity.

It's best to hire someone who is busy, efficient, and engaged, someone who is out there looking at everything and working with all the best craftspeople and showrooms.

Designers have to stay current, otherwise, their work can look dated and dull. Top decorators are constantly on the alert for stimulating ideas around the world. They check out undiscovered resources, view new art, and attend a variety of auctions; they visit both grand and funky antiques galleries; they look for new concepts in fashion, theater sets, and product design. I love to introduce my clients to emerging artists, or a talented craftsperson who is making beautiful hand-blocked wallpapers.

DESIGN AT ITS BEST

Good design often comes down to time and money. I'll always discuss a project's timing and schedule with new clients and work out what can best be accomplished in the available framework. The same goes for decorating on your own—your plan has to be realistic. Clients who want to move in "for a wedding" or "in time for Thanksgiving" are legendary in the design world. Sometimes it can be done, and the party goes on perfectly, as hoped. But there are so many variables—including weather, deliveries, and permits—that I avoid promising a hard-and-fast day for total completion. I'll expedite everything, and I have indeed moved clients in for a special birthday or the holidays, but it's stressful. There are certain things money can't buy, and some things it cannot guarantee.

On the other hand, I can do fast décor when it's required. I have a client who recently acquired a mountain retreat and wanted it ready in just two weeks for a family holiday. I brought all my staff together; we drew on every resource for "off-the-rack" furniture and ready-to-go curtains, bedding, and fittings. We turned to every reliable resource in our books. It was "instant décor," a concept I usually disdain, but we mixed some high-quality antiques and art with the new, and it did not look as if it had all arrived on a truck the same day.

We greeted our clients at the appointed hour with everything in its place, beds made, the refrigerator full, and lunch ready to enjoy. It was a great success, and we flew back to Los Angeles, very relieved and pleased.

Quality takes time. Fine craftsmanship is not something you can hurry. The best custom-made sofas and chairs, couture curtains, and handcrafted cabinets are simply going to take months. We may have to wait for a fabric to be delivered. The studio of a cabinetmaker I like to work with was damaged in a fire. A centuries-old company may suddenly stop weaving a fabric you've used for years. The color of a carpet could be slightly off or wrong. The factory could be closed for the month of August. Mistakes happen.

Unless it's a total rush-rush job, I seldom buy off-the-floor furniture. I have sofas, beds, and chairs custom made. Quality is more important than speed. Most fine craftspeople made names for themselves not by their speed, but by their quality and reliability. The finest designers are usually versatile, and take the same intelligent, perfectionist, and painstaking approach to a range of styles and materials.

My business is built around careful planning. But in the end, inspired design is also about impromptu decisions, spur-of-the-moment choices, and clients' changes of heart. When working on your own or with a designer, it's prudent to consider any new stream of creativity. Have faith in your own taste. Originality appears when you break rules.

Finally, permit yourself to finish the house well. Rooms can be staid, even boring when you do not allow yourself to polish the décor and give the room magic.

The creative process is a fulfilling one. It's thrilling to watch a beautiful room come together, piece by piece. Give yourself time, reject the tried-and-true, and celebrate your personal quirks and interests. Surround yourself with beauty. And never forget to enjoy every room, every day.

Rich in Detail *Opposite:* Working with Los Angeles architect Mark Rios, Smith added detail and a voluptuous sensuality to the former shell of a house to replicate the individuality and heritage of a Tuscan villa. A turned bedpost affords a sense of architectural detail, alongside an antique Venetian chair. The colors are opulent but muted, as if faded over time.

FINDING AND WORKING WITH A DECORATOR

Engaging and working with a top decorator sounds like the easiest—and happiest—of design projects, but it's one that requires careful thought and research. Begin the process by clipping images of rooms you love from magazines. Designers should be brought in early in the planning stages of a new house, rather than after the interior architecture decisions have been made.

When you're first considering hiring a decorator, talk to friends, antiques dealers, contractors, and architects about designers they've worked with, know, and admire. If you have access to to-the-trade showrooms, speak to the manager about designer referrals.

Visit decorator showcase houses and design-oriented events, and look for designers' vignettes or presentations at leading antiques shows (like those in San Francisco, New York, and Los Angeles) and design charity events. At decorator showcases, designers often present their best work, free of the constraints of budgets and clients.

Friends are an especially good resource. Ask about designers they've worked with, consider their observation, and gauge their satisfaction. Was the designer punctual, easy to contact, and reliable? Was the firm candid regarding budgets and costs? Did they manage the project well and in a timely manner? Was the designer open to ideas and

---

A Working Relationship *Above:* In collaboration with Los Angeles architects, Tichenor & Thorp, and owners Gary and Maria Gersh, Michael Smith designed a room of eclectic art and furniture. The result of a professional team's expertise: a cozy, polished room with an updated, traditional feeling that works for a family.

Opposite: Smith selected an antique leather chest and rug to add a romantic feeling to a characterless brand-new "builder Mediterranean" house in Malibu. The walls were covered in squares of birch bark to give complexity and texture to the under-detailed walls.

suggestions? Was the principal designer easy to work with, or did assistants handle most of the work?

It's important to find someone you like, a designer whose aesthetic judgment you trust. Hire someone whose work you've admired over time—a professional who is talented, versatile, and organized, and who takes you seriously.

Potential clients should know what they love, and what they can't abide. My ideal prospective client comes to the interview clear on the scope of the project but open-minded and flexible when it comes to the details.

The job of a designer is to provide options and to broaden the scope of possibilities.

If I were going to hire a decorator I'd want to know that they have a top-notch accounting process, and a meticulous bookkeeping department. All transactions should be clear, orderly, and timely, as with every professional.

I recommend contacting two or three designers you'd like to interview. Discuss the project and the budget candidly, and find out what the designer can and cannot do within a given time frame. Designers want to be assured that clients understand the reality of the time it takes to complete a project, and can work with a sensible budget. Bring along the clippings of images of rooms that you like. It's a good way to communicate your taste, and a way for you and the designer to know if it's a good match.

Consider the possibility of working with a designer from another city. Today's designers are adept at working all over the world. Most leading firms are set up to work for their clients wherever they live, wherever they may acquire a new residence, or set up a pied-à-terre in another city across the country. At any time my staff and I may be working on houses in Los Angeles, Bozeman, Montana, London, New York, Santa Barbara, and the Hawaiian Islands. Clients are just a phone call, e-mail, or fax away. We have endless resources in every city, and work with leading architects in each location.

GETTING TO KNOW YOU

A good decorator wants to understand the client's expectations. If possible, the designer should go and view the house or apartment, or see plans for a new residence. That said, sometimes good chemistry is undeniable. I have had clients whose enthusiasm and concepts were so engaging that I said "yes" without even seeing the house. They knew my work and we had an instant rapport.

Designer friends of mine tell me that, like me, they prefer to have a close relationship with their clients. They also appreciate it when clients are involved and pay attention to the design process. Designers love enthusiasm. It's gratifying to see clients who are truly pleased with their new rooms—clients who understand, and appreciate what has been created for them.

Ideally your designer should meet the architects and builders of a new house to discuss working together to make your dream come alive.

If it seems that I am not the right person for a particular client, I am delighted to refer them to another architect or a designer I'm familiar with and admire.

There are two key points in going forward. One is mutual trust; the other is a spirit of cooperation between the client and the designer. Good design requires a professional and emotional investment. I don't ever want to do a less than perfect job. The client has to stay the course, too, and maintain his or her interest. People who are serious about design make a commitment.

It is obviously very personal to work on a client's house and spend their money. Because of this, I would do anything to help them. I've organized weddings. I've lent my own furniture for a party. For some clients, I've purchased everything from Picassos to vacuum cleaners. I've painted over walls at my own expense when a color I recommended proved to be a disappointment. I've traveled at the last minute to prepare a house for a special event.

Ideally, my clients and I develop a great rapport, a fine friendship, and a warm and constructive understanding. My staff and I work on multiple houses for longtime clients. We'll complete their business offices, design the interiors of their private planes, and then work on their children's houses, guesthouses, or vacation homes. I respect their budgets. Some clients want to collect the finest antiques and art, and others are more cost-conscious. Sometimes there is a change of plan for practical reasons. Designers should be flexible and fair. It's always a great moment when my client and I come to an agreement, sign the contracts, and move forward with the design process.

GETTING STARTED

At the first in-office meeting, after contracts have been signed, we'll discuss some proposals, we'll look at images of furniture and art, and we'll discuss the project's design and timing in a loose way. We'll also look at practical aspects, such as do they want a formal dining room, how many bedrooms and guest rooms will there be, and design requirements for a home office, library, or kitchen. We'll review any plans for remodeling, additions, or renovation. Then we'll meet with the architect or contractor, and start to formulate a clear plan, and a working timetable.

I get to know my clients' likes and dislikes, their interests, and their passions. I need to know how clients like to spend their time, where they read, where their children do their homework, where the family likes to gather. I start to develop a blueprint in my mind.

I'll make a first design proposal based on this infor-

mation and discussions with the architect. For some clients, I may develop elevations, drawings, and quite detailed descriptions. For others it's somewhat more open-ended.

With plans in place, and a design agreed upon, my clients will sign off on purchases and made-to-order designs. I commission the custom-made furniture, curtains, and carpets.

Timing varies with each project, and with the complexity of each house. Sometimes we wait for planning approval, which can delay us for months. Or we wait for custom-crafted carpets, trim, or silk.

Certain plans which do not involve custom work can be accomplished very fast, thanks to showrooms, Pottery Barn, mail-order catalogs, Target (yes, Target), and leading

design stores that stock goods for immediate delivery.

A job can take anywhere from several days to several years. A city pied-à-terre may be perfected in just a few months (even with trips to Paris to find antiques), while a large, brand-new Connecticut family house with stables, barns, and guesthouses can take years from start to finish. My firm is very flexible, and we love to rise to a challenge.

Some of my clients are hands-on, and get closely involved in each purchase. We may make plans to visit art and antiques dealers in New York, Antwerp, Paris, or London to find unique pieces. Other clients want me to make the selections, with their approval. I love all ways of working.

We share a common goal. The great design begins.

Pale Beauty *Above:* A calm and superbly composed interior was created with a deft juxtaposition of capacious armchairs and refined pale wood chairs, along with well-chosen antiques and tranquil paintings in rich gilded frames.

When working with an architect, interior designer, contractor, landscape designer, or craftsperson:

- Be clear and communicative about expectations and desires.

- Do your homework. Know what you like and what you don't like. Be clear on your needs—from wine storage to shelves for your collection of first editions; from dog beds to closet space; from bathroom lighting to a home office.

- Pay attention, take notes, and listen. Be willing to perhaps expand your original plan to make it better, bigger, and more satisfying.

- You'll be working directly with the designer, who will in turn work directly with a team of specialists, from design assistants to general contractors or architects, tile-layers, painters, and many craftspeople. The designer will also be ordering fabrics, working with showrooms, and juggling every aspect of the project. Mistakes can happen. Custom-crafted goods invite the possibility of error: an incorrect measurement or color, a misunderstanding, the wrong beige, a toast-colored wall covering instead of rich cream. It's important to have a sense of humor and trust that the designer will make it all work out.

- Stick to your guns. Allowing yourself to be talked into something you don't like—only to decide later you can't live with it—can be disastrous. Avoid being wishy-washy and indecisive, and especially don't change your mind repeatedly. It's unnerving to the designer and it can be a nightmare when plans, paint, plumbing, plaster, or tile work has to be redone.

- An architect or designer is an advisor who does not, ultimately, have the final decision. They do not sign the checks; you do.

- It's a creative process. Stay the course, and remain emotionally involved.

- Observe with optimism. Be patient. Creative people are working hard to make you happy. Don't antagonize the decorator, and always assume the best.

- Pay in a timely and considerate manner.

- Be accountable to all your decisions. Don't rush out and buy major antiques, furniture, or art without first discussing it with your designer.

- Be cautious and pay attention. Try out fabric samples, paint swatches, and furniture pieces to ensure that you can live with them. For example, I recommend having two dining room chair samples brought in, if possible. It's easier to imagine ten chairs with two in front of you. Spend a week living with a painting or a sculpture. Spontaneity is fine, but it's best not to rush major decisions.

- Minimize the element of surprise. Don't make decisions without considering all aspects of the design.

- If you are not comfortable with a designer's plans or decisions, make a graceful exit only after considerable thought. Keep the parting amicable and perhaps even open-ended.

- Your taste should not be steamrolled, but it is also not your job to demean the designer, his or her staff, and their taste or ideas. The goal is to create beautiful rooms; it's not a challenge to see who "wins" every decision.

- Try not to comment until everything is in place: that is, until the rooms are finished, and the furniture is correctly placed. Don't stand by the truck and critique. Look at everything in context. A sense of truly "working together" makes a project go well.

Today, the design process is a democratic one. The days of the decorator as a tyrant or dictator, with a mean poodle in the back of a Rolls-Royce convertible, are over. The designer autocrat made for very unhappy clients and sad endings. Design is now a collaborative process. Clients feel free to voice their concerns. It can be stressful (when it's pouring rain and a new house still lacks a roof, or when a paint color turns out muddy and depressing), but with excellent communication, all problems can be solved.

BUYING ANTIQUES

Fine, rare, and eccentric antiques have been part of my life since I was young. Today, my antiques acquisitions are wide-ranging and ever-changing, and grounded in more than two decades of observation and study. My purchases are driven by my passion for antiques, craftsmanship, and art in all their guises and forms.

I have learned from legendary dealers such as Carlton Hobbs, Joel Chen, Amy Perlin, Ariane Dandois, and Axel Vervoordt. I relish oddity and idiosyncrasy: the superb simplicity of a Shaker or Nakashima table; the wildness of a gilt rococo Venetian mirror. Wherever I am, I look for quality and originality—a Charlotte Perriand chair, a seventies plastic chair prototype, a Dupré-Lafon lamp, a sixteenth-century framed Korean map, or a Japanese screen.

In Los Angeles, I recently found a great Pierre Cardin brass coffee table from the sixties. Regardless of where you look, the key to finding treasures in lofty antiques galleries

and caviar-fueled art fairs, as well as at down-and-dusty flea markets, specialist auctions, and street fairs, is to be enthusiastic, curious, and open-minded.

An entire shop crammed to the rafters with fine antiques can be daunting. An antiques gallery or vintage store with just a few finely edited and curated objects can be even more intimidating. Have courage. Approach buying antiques as a wonderful adventure. In the store, a scholarly approach is appropriate, but so is a simple appreciation of the beauty of decorative objects and fine paintings.

For antiques beginners, I urge you to start by attending lectures and seminars, poring over auction catalogs, and looking closely at the pieces offered for sale.

Begin with perhaps a small table, an ottoman, a fifties lamp, a sixties Italian chair prototype, or a pair of Moroccan pottery urns. Try not to anticipate—you may search for a mahogany sideboard and find instead a glorious painted

Sumptuous Contrasts *Above:* To create a mood of silken beauty and polish for an office in the heart of Hollywood, Michael Smith brought together a Biedermeier pedestal table from Niall Smith in New York, and a pair of Northern Italian antique chairs from Therien & Co., in Los Angeles. To underplay the luxury, colors were creamy, pale, and controlled. *Opposite:* In Southern California, the designer created a harmonious corner with a slip-covered settee, a gold-framed plein air painting, and an antique Continental table that's just the perfect height for taking tea or a glass of wine with guests. *Following pages:* Several trips to Paris, London, and New York—as well as visits to top antiques dealers on La Cienega Boulevard in Los Angeles—produced the luxe neoclassical chairs and tables, antique Chinese blue-and-white porcelain urns, and eighteenth-century English gilt mirrors in this Los Angeles entry hall.

hope chest. Inspect the furniture from all angles. Ask the dealer to turn chairs and tables (and even sofas) upside down so that the tacks and construction and any over-painting or repairs can be viewed.

Sit on chairs to be sure they are stable and reasonably comfortable.

Discuss any restorations that have been made, and the cost of any needed repairs, regilding, or new upholstery, which can be quite pricey. Consult with a specialist before making any alterations, since certain changes may affect the value of the piece.

Learn everything you can. Buy the best quality you can afford. Craftsmanship never goes out of style.

Antiques bring so much to a room and work with everything. It's never the pair of eighteenth-century gilt consoles, the Chinese chair, the thirties desk lamp, or the quirky Georgian chairs you sell when moving. They are lifelong friends. You don't tire of your beloved English writing table, a French forties glass vase, a mid-century industrial lamp, or humble Japanese bowl. They only get better over the years.

That doesn't mean it's necessary to aim for museum-like authenticity in every room. Interiors full of precious antiques or unused vintage fifties pieces feel like a museum, not a home.

Antiques and vintage pieces benefit from contrast and juxtaposition. It's best to mix periods. Standing a curvy Gio Ponti steel chair beside a sculptural black-lacquered eighteenth-century Chinese altar table, or hanging an ornate glittery Line Vautrin mirror above a neoclassical console by André Arbus, shows them all to advantage. Don't be afraid to enjoy your favorite pieces every day. Antiques and great vintage finds should be used, so that they become like old friends.

A Light Hand *Above and Opposite:* For leading director/producer Jerry Zucker in Los Angeles, Smith kept the living room colors strictly pale and low-key, as a canvas for an antique Swedish painted chair, an upholstered Biedermeier wing chair, a Picasso etching, and a glamorous antique Venetian painted table. Diversity and variety serve the antiques and the room well.

Creamy Surroundings *Following pages:* For hotelier/restaurateur Peter Morton's house in Los Angeles, Smith selected an antique Russian chair from Ariane Dandois in Paris, a Jean-Michel Frank–style coffee table, and a richly detailed nineteenth-century Indian carpet. The curtains, in the classic Michael Smith style, are simple yet luxuriant.

FAVORITE SOURCES FOR ANTIQUES AND VINTAGE PIECES

I've been buying antiques for two decades, and have always relied on major auction houses and venerable dealers.

Sources are becoming more diverse, and new specialists seem to appear every few months. The world of collecting and buying vintage and antiques is now completely universal. Between the Internet, international flights, FedEx, shipping services, and faxes and e-mails, everyone and everything is within reach.

In addition to Christie's, Sotheby's, and Phillips, I have been working with Wright auctions in Chicago, which specialize in twentieth-century design. For excellent selections of Arts & Crafts, Danish Modern, and twentieth-century designs, I check on Treadway Galleries in Cincinnati.

I've acquired French antiques and paintings from Etude Tajan in Paris; at Bukowski in Stockholm I've found outstanding Swedish wool carpets and a selection of flat-weaves and Oriental rugs and carpets. Skinner in Boston is action central for antique and vintage American furniture and decorative arts, European paintings, and Asian works of art. Northeast Auctions in New Hampshire offers fine antique American and European furniture and decorative objects.

In London, Paris, or Antwerp, I explore the city in hopes of finding an unknown gallery, a just-opened antiques shop, or a hidden vintage atelier. Even in a not-so-great shop, I hope to uncover a treasure.

In New York, I roam through all the neighborhoods in search of the next talented dealer, the latest gallery, or a pioneer on an edgy street. Franklin Street in TriBeCa has an eclectic group of shops, and I particularly like Antik, which sells Scandinavian vintage furniture, as well as studio ceramics from the thirties, forties, and fifties.

Uptown, on East 57th Street in Manhattan, I go to the William Lipton gallery, which specializes in Chinese furniture and Pan-Asian works of art. Also on 57th Street is M.D. Flacks, a noted specialist in classical Chinese furniture. De Lorenzo on Lafayette Street is a reliable source for twentieth-century classics and iconic modern designs.

Back home in Los Angeles, I often stop by Blackman Cruz, on La Cienega Boulevard—which offers a mix of furnishings with great presence—and at Downtown, on the same street. On Main Street, in Venice, California (not far from my office), I stop in at Obsolete for quirky American furniture, paintings, and sculptural found objects. The owners have a passion for discovering mysterious objects, nothing ordinary.

There are always "bedrock" pieces I'm looking for, and I recommend that collectors keep an eye out for both basic and classic pieces, along with the rare and extraordinary. I'm on the hunt for Chippendale chairs, as well as blanc de chine. You can't argue, you'll always want these beautiful, timeless pieces.

New ideas and concepts can spring up at flea markets, on the street, in obscure publications, at auction, and at museum shows and gallery collections. It's important to be in touch with the zeitgeist, to look with an open mind and stay nonjudgmental at first. For example, be inspired by the California interior designer Frances Elkins, who bought Jean-Michel Frank furniture in Paris in the thirties and commissioned tables and lamps from Giacometti in the forties. She also confidently pioneered the concept of combining rich and rare antiques with inexpensive pictures and objects. A favorite conceit is massing the gilt-framed cutout prints she's found in Paris on the walls of her adobe in Monterey.

It's the search that I love. Meeting dealers, bidding at auction, driving out of my way to see a new gallery in Chelsea or Chicago, or getting up at the crack of dawn to go to the flea markets in Paris is tremendously fulfilling. I'm always learning, always looking—and often finding. There are few better ways to spend time.

Details, Details *Opposite:* In the de Rothschild entry hall in the family's New York apartment, a grouping of rare Chinese porcelains are clustered on a French neoclassical table from Carlton Hobbs.

THE JOY OF AUCTIONS

Until recently, auctions were primarily known to the design trade, dealers, serious collectors, and insiders who had the know-how and confidence to circumnavigate the rules and the arcane language of auction catalogs and sales.

With increasing interest in antiques and art collecting, auctions have become more accessible to the general public. They are an important source for fine antiques, rare book collections, paintings, and photography, as well as obscure and exceptional sculptures, textiles, carpets, and porcelains.

Now anyone interested in collecting art and antiques can subscribe to auction catalogs and attend auctions. With this increased openness in the auction process, collectors can bid in person, on the telephone, or over the Internet.

Thanks to recent high-profile antiques and art sales like those showcasing the estates and collections of such connoisseurs as Jacqueline Kennedy Onassis, Carlos de Bestegui, Michael Taylor, Marella Agnelli, Pamela Harriman, Madeleine Castaing, and Karl Lagerfeld, auctions are more enticing and glamorous. Those who love decorative arts with a connection to history can learn to find fantastic treasures.

Also new on the scene are a lively group of small regional auction houses which specialize in twentieth-century furniture, antique glass, jewelry, Hollywood artifacts and style, and Americana. These are great places to discover the unknown artists, hard-to-find Mid-Century Modern design, obscure photography, and intriguing found objects that add

Classic Hollywood *Opposite:* In a thirties Los Angeles house, the designer kept antiques and art glamorous and elegant, but not elaborate. An eighteenth-century English gilt chair, acquired at auction, contrasts with a pair of antique Spanish console tables won at a Sotheby's auction. Colors are muted and soft, to allow the antiques and the architectural detail to take center stage. *Above:* Michael Smith finds auctions a valuable source of many design items, and enriches his interiors with antique textiles from around the world, mirrors, lighting, architectural details and fragments, and even stone mantels, tiles, marble tabletops, and ceramics. A well-focused, attentive, and passionate collector can find auctions a valuable and sometimes addictive source of surprising treasures, often at bargain prices.

such character and texture to interiors.

Auctions around the world and across the United States offer a fascinating grab bag of good—sometimes great—antiques which can often be acquired for a very reasonable price.

With many auctions, this may be the first time items like a fine antique Venetian console, a George Nakashima table, or a Samuel Marx parchment chest may be coming onto the market. It's a wonderful game to search for the world's best antiques, and serious collectors, decorators, and dealers can get first pick.

With a willing seller and a lucky buyer, there's a chance of finding a brilliant piece at a bargain price. On the other hand, it only takes two very passionate and enthusiastic bidders to drive prices sky high, especially at an auction with a celebrity attached. Provenance is the wild card of auctions. At an auction of a famous person's estate (think the Duchess of Windsor or Bill Blass), there's a frenzy to own one of his or her paintings or chairs or rugs. A table that belonged to Maria Callas, or a mirror by French designer Line Vautrin,

becomes magical. It's easy to get carried away when you find something you love. Be disciplined.

Auction houses publish glossy catalogs for all sales. They are full of information about antiques, and are a useful reference. I subscribe to catalogs from Denmark, Sweden, Germany, Belgium, and France, as well as from throughout the United States. Every weekend, I read through at least a dozen catalogs, especially during the fall and early summer sale seasons. Through a variety of auctions you have access to nationwide and worldwide collections, making your possible selections infinitely more cosmopolitan. Through careful study, you can become an expert on Swedish neoclassicism or Moroccan carpets, for example. Your taste and knowledge broaden. It's inspiring to read about beautiful things in a wide range of styles and designs, and to get caught up in the history and tradition of interiors and antiques.

Keep important catalogs for reference, and use them to compare prices along with the quality and contents of special collections.

Deft Contrasts *Above and Opposite:* A pair of voluptuous Persian urns found at auction in Los Angeles contrast with an angular thirties desk lamp on a carved Indian console. The red peonies in a crystal vase are a cheerful design flourish. In the modernist living room of his Santa Monica penthouse, Michael Smith mixed a tin-covered wood table handcrafted in Rajasthan (an auction find) and an Italian chair covered in Indian hand-blocked cotton. The sofa, covered in striped silk, is a Michael Smith design.

NAVIGATING AUCTIONS

I've always loved the excitement of special auctions. The atmosphere is charged with passion and expectation. Some bidders are impulsive, others determined to find their heart's desire.

Recently at a London auction, I wanted to acquire an eighteenth-century Murano mirror in clear and blue glass. This exquisite mirror was octagonal, but simple in its design. It was palazzo scale, and very expensive. I set myself a limit beyond which I would not bid, and I stuck to it. Unfortunately, someone else wanted it more than I, and they won with a higher bid.

That's the way it is with auctions, whether it's a rug auction in San Francisco, an estate sale in Pennsylvania, a rainy-day auction in Paris, or a glamorous sale in New York. You're bidding against others who may have a larger budget— or who may simply be desperate for that particular item. Stay within the limits that you set yourself.

However, be open-minded about beautiful things out- side your special interest. For instance, I found a rare and important Richard Diebenkorn drawing, which no one else seemed to have noticed or liked.

And at a recent sale in North Carolina, I found a stack of wood piled on the auction house floor. It looked like junk, until I noticed its beautiful carved moldings. There was little information on this "lumber," and no diagrams or directions for reassembling it. It was simply billed as "a 19th-century pine room."

I saw the quality of the carving and knew it would be a valuable purchase, but I got it for a fair price. I later discov- ered it is hemlock, and in beautiful condition. I gave it a very subtle beeswax finish and my bedroom walls in Bel-Air are now panelled in it—it is simply exquisite.

It pays to be focused. Pick an area of interest—archi- tectural drawings, blue-and-white porcelain urns, antique Turkish textiles or Georgian candlesticks—learn all you can about it, and then keep your eyes open. You'll be surprised by how quickly you can become an expert and develop your collection.

Reading the Classics *Above:* A Regency book cabinet in macassar wood, acquired at a London auction, is brought together with a worldly collection of a Chinese terra- cotta camel, a nineteenth-century French terra-cotta figure clock, and paintings found at Paris and New York auctions. Michael Smith's credo: Don't over-arrange objects, and keep flowers graceful and understated. *Opposite:* In a Los Angeles residence, a pair of neoclassical Italian chairs flank an early-nineteenth-century French writing desk with ormolu mounts, all auction trophies. To find and win such treasures, Smith insists, it is important to study auction catalogs carefully, bid prudently, and never bid on high-ticket items which have not been personally inspected.

VIEWING AND STUDYING

It is essential to view in person all pieces you plan to bid on, so there will be no surprises. Selecting an antique based solely on a photograph, without carefully checking dimensions, and reading a complete condition report, can lead to disappointment.

First, read the catalogs carefully and in detail. Study the glossary of descriptions, and understand the difference between "in the style of" or "from the school of," "from the studio of" or "attributed to," "similar to" or "thought to be." Auction house specialists, using their best information and knowledge, may be offering inaccurate or perhaps optimistic descriptions. Bidder, beware.

Focus carefully on pieces you need and want. Understand the field, and consider the rarity of pieces you like. Compare them with online auctions and scan comparable auctions and realized prices. Haunt the sales for a few months before bidding.

Talk to the auction house specialists. Discuss auction protocol. Ask about the process from start to hammer fall, including auction house premiums (percentages charged by auction houses on sales) and legal aspects of a sale.

Ask questions about a piece's history, origin, condition, and any restoration or repairs, as well as the craftsman or artist. Check for clarification on the estimated price. Request details on fixes and possible additions. A gilt Venetian console table, for example, may have a marble top that was added later. A beautiful rug might have been repaired. Table legs may have been cut down, or entirely new legs added to a chair. Newer upholstery may have replaced the original tapestry or silk damask on an antique chair. New paint, in a more modern color, may have been added over the original to make a chair more saleable and appealing to a modern audience.

Ask permission to turn chairs upside down, to check their condition or find any stamps or signatures. I suggest that you run your fingers across tabletops, inspect the undersides of

Bold Design Strokes *Opposite:* An 8-foot-tall allegorical painting, from the school of Rubens, bought at a Sotheby's auction, creates drama and tension in Smith's Los Angeles bedroom. On the bed: an antique *suzani*, a favorite graphic textile. The chaise longue was designed by T.H. Robsjohn-Gibbings in 1961, after a design he found on a 400 B.C. painted Greek vase. The television is left in full view. The new and the ancient worlds come together here. "When appropriate, the television is less intrusive simply standing on a table than hidden in a large armoire," said the designer. "In this case, in my own bedroom, I preferred it with no flourishes and no disguise. It is a fact of modern life."

Auction Treasures and Rare Finds *Opposite:* An allegorical painting, attributed to Tintoretto, from the Hackwood Hall country house sale, offers its gilt presence with a painted Italian bench and a Régence gilt chair covered in saddle-colored leather. The chair was formerly the property of "Babe" Paley. *Above (clockwise from top left):* An apartment in Manhattan is graced with an ormolu photofore on a neoclassical French center table. Beside it, a collection of Egyptian antiquities from Christie's and Sotheby's; A Korean box stands on a Japanese table, acquired from Bonham's auction house; An eighteenth-century French armillary and an antique globe were Paris auction house acquisitions; An Imari vase with ormolu mounts accompanies an ormolu candlestick, and a Blue John stone urn in a neoclassical form with ormolu mounts.

chairs and tables, and carefully examine carpets. Do the same kind of due diligence with stemware (run your fingers around the rims), and with pottery or crystal.

Take a measuring tape to check dimensions of all furniture and paintings. Be sure a piece will not only fit in the intended position in a room, but also through the doorway or into an apartment building elevator.

Use a magnifying glass to inspect a canvas or a photograph. Often a closer look may reveal fading, sun damage, cracking, or repairs that can affect its value. Check the backs of paintings, prints, and photographs to be sure canvases have not been trimmed, and to note dimensions and conditions of paper and canvas.

At home, conduct more research on pieces on which

you'd like to bid. Learn more on the work of Jean Prouvé, or Chinese porcelains, or Alvar Aalto chairs, or Georgian silver, for example.

I recommend establishing a relationship with a local auction house and its specialists. Get to know the vocabulary of sales and antiques and vintage designs; the people; the added fees; and the timing and pattern of bidding.

In the end, protect yourself and maintain discipline by establishing your price and sticking to it. Know when to go over your budget (perhaps for a one-of-a-kind object with an impeccable provenance), and when to stick to your limit.

Know that there will always be tantalizing auctions in the next season, or the following year. My motto is, "There will always be more beautiful things."

The Dance of Time *Opposite:* A Regency penwork chair, from a London auction, stands before a honed black marble fireplace in Beverly Hills. Renzo Mongiardino designed the pair of rare specimen marble plinths. *Above:* In the same hillside residence of an acclaimed television writer/producer and his wife, a pair of French marble bas-reliefs and a carved Regency chair covered in natural-colored horsehair, add richness and texture to a monochromatic room.

ONLINE AUCTIONS

Online auctions can be an excellent resource if you understand how they work, and if you do extensive and careful research on dealers, sources, descriptions, and prices. These Internet auctions also give you access to smaller dealers, specialists, and passionate collectors around the world.

Exercise caution and care. It doesn't take long to become addicted to the apparent ease of buying or bidding over the Internet, and it can appear far simpler than it is.

When starting out, it is usually wise to be able to inspect pieces in person. Measure and appraise, and then make your decision. On the other hand, I've made some excellent buys of well-priced architectural prints, decorative objects, and ceramics online, sight unseen.

From eBay, I've acquired porcelains from Shanghai dealers, as well as thirties Adirondack camp furniture, antique textiles, great Mid-Century Modern lighting, and unusual fifties cabinets and chairs.

I also work with 1stdibs.com (based in Paris and the Hamptons) to find antiques and vintage pieces. In addition, at lotfinder.com, I've made some good discoveries.

I also use the Internet to conduct research on a variety of auctions, special sales, and antiques shows.

Grace and Favor *Opposite:* In a Los Angeles entry hall, a Regency mirror swirls its carved and gilt frame above a Georgian viburnum table. While such treasures may not often appear in online auctions, silver candlesticks and Chinese export porcelain vases (here made into a lamp) may be found online. *Above:* In a Beverly Hills dining room, a Georgian sideboard was found at a live auction. Chic crystal sconces, however, were bid on and won from 1stdibs.com. The wallpaper is by de Gournay.

THE VIRTUOSO ANTIQUES DEALER

I have been obsessed with antiques and art for most of my life. When I was still in high school, I would visit antiques shops and galleries in Southern California. I chatted with dealers and got to know both them and their wares. I would visit antiques shops to buy and to observe dealers in action. I later worked with noted San Juan Capistrano antiquarian Gep Durenberger, and traveled to London and New York with him to appraise, view, and purchase antiques. I also learned firsthand about antiques and fine art from visits to Evans & Gerst in Long Beach. These experiences taught me to be a decisive, confident, and independent buyer, and later as a designer I applied this knowledge to serve my clients' needs.

When I started my design career, I relied on many dealers in Los Angeles, and gained the confidence to start buying in Europe. When I was studying design and antiques in London, I began to haunt antiques and design firms like Colefax & Fowler. I explored the glories of Pimlico Road as well as the notable shops along Fulham Road. Two decades later, I am acquainted with many of the world's top dealers, and often drop in to visit them when I am in London, Paris, New York, Los Angeles, and Antwerp. I depend on a network of a variety of dealers to inform me of new arrivals, a great vintage sale, new artists, and collections on view. Working closely with specialists in a broad range of fields, I have great respect for their superb taste and arcane sources,

Confident Style, Great Sources *Opposite:* In a New York duplex overlooking the East River, Michael Smith brought together a virtuoso composition of a mid-nineteenth-century mahogany dining table from Christopher Hodsoll and a series of handsome Georgian-style chairs. Silver photofores, cloisonné bowls, seasonal peonies in full bloom, and family silver collections add luster. The eighteenth-century wallpaper was acquired at Sotheby's, London.

their rich knowledge and keen appraisals.

In my work it's important to stay fresh. Any serious collector therefore, should search a range of galleries, antiques shows, fairs, shops, and emerging neighborhoods. I've found some of my favorite things in unlikely places: a street market in London, a hidden corner of SoHo, a quiet street in Antwerp.

Beautiful things are not always the most expensive or precious, and the best antiques are not always at the glitziest dealers' galleries. I look at every level. I'm not just obsessed with the most precious pieces. I'm more interested in the look and impact of furniture and objects, and sometimes the best pieces are the bargains.

I can get inspiration going to an American art fair in Farmington, Connecticut, at 7:30 A.M. looking for painted furniture, or finding a talented new vintage dealer in Venice, California. I'll attend a Modernism show in Palm Springs, look for folk art in Pennsylvania, spend two days walking the aisles at the great Maastricht international fine arts and antiques fair in the Netherlands, or attend the Olympia antiques and art

show in London. At the same time, I will stay attuned to a new dealer with a tiny shop in Hudson, New York, or a Los Angeles specialist in twentieth-century design who has a good eye. If only I had enough time, I'd fly to Bangkok or Istanbul to find specialist dealers in textiles or decorative objects there, too. Make collecting a great adventure.

Dealers and specialists play an essential role in my search for beautiful things. From my very first days as a young decorator, I've always enjoyed great relationships and camaraderie with top specialist dealers—of rugs, paintings, antiques, photography, textiles, and decorative arts and objects.

The most successful dealers have great taste and discernment, as well as a thorough knowledge of their fields. Nothing can replace their editing, their eye, their insight, their ability to identify rare and exceptional antiques and art. I admire passionate dealers who really and truly believe in everything they're selling. Watching them at work, observing their enthusiasm, presentation, and style around such valuable objects, is truly inspiring.

Great dealers understand fine craftsmanship: the

The Pleasures of Contrast and Surprise *Opposite:* A circa 1860 grain-painted chest of drawers makes a fine companion to an Arts & Crafts clock and a California plein-air painting with its original gold frame. Smith's flower style in this composition: fresh and unpretentious flowers in a simple glass column vase. *Above:* In a corner of a bedroom in Santa Ynez, California, an eighteenth-century Italian cabinet inlaid with rare marble specimens makes a stage for handsome sang-de-boeuf Chinese vases.

history of art and furniture making, the lives and biographies of fine furniture makers and great painters. The best dealers I know can look beyond what is fashionable and view antique pieces and art from a timeless, classic perspective. They see the big picture of antiques and art history, the world of creation.

In my design work, I'm seldom looking for anything trendy, but dealers will often research and find obscure yet wonderful work. They will introduce me to a new artist, unearth an unknown but terrific designer, or discover an up-and-coming photographer or a neglected painter. The finest dealers transcend current tastes and fads. They have great insight into beauty in all its forms, and will have their antennae finely tuned to discern where the markets are going next. They'll catch a new trend or direction before anyone else sees it.

I have great respect for antiques specialists, and listen to their directions and opinions in a variety of fields and areas of expertise. They help me navigate the waters, and they often have an awareness far ahead of buyers. They see pieces before they come onto the market, and often find types of antiques that had been neglected or are out of favor, like Napoléon III or early Biedermeier pieces. They'll know when it's time to present them, and can advise on when the time is right for buying them. Top dealers in antiques and vintage pieces understand the zeitgeist, and can feel changes in the air before they're truly apparent. Good dealers embrace antiques and art that may at first seem awkward or difficult, but they have the authority to make you pay attention. This is especially true for dealers in twentieth-century design, who may have unearthed neglected seventies furniture designs that can look raw or outra-geous at first glance. A great dealer can force you to stop, take a second look, learn, and perhaps appreciate.

Antiques and art dealing is the last gentlemanly profession (I should note that some of my favorite and most admired dealers, like Ariane Dandois and Amy Perlin, are women), and it works in the most extraordinary manner, like no other profession.

I've taken a million-dollar antique out of a gallery on approval—on a handshake and a signature. Of course, I ended up purchasing the piece, but this was a transaction based purely on trust.

I work with wonderful dealers at every level of the antiques business. I have had relationships for many years with fine dealers at the Paris flea markets (like the Paul Bert and Serpette markets at the Porte de Clignancourt) who often find the best antiques "in their juice" from estates before anyone else. For my clients, I also work with the top dealers in London and New York. We'll fly in to Antwerp to visit the great Axel Vervoordt, or stop in London to see Carlton Hobbs.

Dealers I love include Carlton Hobbs in London and New York. His spheres of interest include sculptural and architectural furniture, which I collect. His pieces are of extraordinary rarity. They are dramatic and beautiful. He's the real deal.

In London, I haunt Hemisphere, along with Sibyll Colefax and John Fowler, Mallett, Piers von Westenholz, John Hobbs, Christopher Gibbs, and Christopher Hodsoll.

In New York, I have many favorite dealers. Among them are Amy Perlin (who works very hard, travels constantly, and has an amazing eye), Louis Bofferding (who has a fantastic and scholarly knowledge of great twentieth-

---

Provenance and Assurance *Opposite:* For a family room paneled in eucalyptus wood, Smith selected a Mahal carpet from Mansour in London. The Italian chair was from Joel Chen, one of Smith's favorite Los Angeles dealers. The round Spanish games table was from Fremontier, an antiques dealer on the quai Voltaire in Paris, which specializes in pieces from the seventeenth to the twentieth century.

century architects, decorators, and furniture), Niall Smith, Kentshire, and H.M. Luther. I'm always looking for eclectic and special decorative objects that have great presence, and I rely on these dealers to show them and find them.

In Los Angeles I like to work with Joel Chen, Paul Ferrante, Lee Stanton, and Therien & Co.

Dealers can help educate new collectors and enrich the knowledge of serious buyers. I recommend visiting them in their galleries, and following them to annual and biannual antiques shows where they show their finest collections and treasured pieces. Smaller ceramics, textiles, pillows, and bronzes can be found at reasonable prices.

In an ongoing antiques education, it's wise to attend seminars and museum lectures, spend Saturdays visiting antiques and art galleries, gather a range of guides and reference books and catalogs, and to look at everything you can. It's also essential to start your own collection of reference books for your areas of interest so that you can collect with discernment. Ask specialist dealers for their recommendations of authoritative books.

Over time, the dealers you patronize will become friends who will deepen your knowledge and expertise. As your appreciation and understanding grows, you will broaden your horizons and your taste, and you will enjoy antiques and art more and more.

Interiors with Character *Top left:* In Neil and Francine Afromsky's Santa Ynez villa, an eighteenth-century map on parchment forms a background for a seventeenth-century bronze figure acquired in Italy. *Left:* An Art Deco blue-glass framed mirror, contrasts with a Chinese burlwood console, both from the Los Angeles antiques dealer Joel Chen. Smith selected these pieces for Brian Grazer and Gigi Levangie Grazer's beach house. The amber drinking glasses, used as candle votives, are from Ikea. *Opposite:* Gigi Levangie Grazer's study in Malibu features a Malevich-inspired glass-topped table from the Michael Smith Collection.

PAINT: STYLE ENHANCER AND MOOD MAKER

I have spent countless hours planning, designing, selecting, reviewing, and confirming paint colors. I have learned that the best color schemes are often the result of both careful deliberation and a dash of bravado.

I have relished experimenting with eccentric and dramatic and "off" colors to get certain effects in my own apartments and houses over the years, but I proceed with more care, deliberation, and patience when choosing colors for my clients.

Color selection is an art. There are no absolute rules and the old design concepts can seem rather dated; they were so rigid. Color selection today is much more personal and idiosyncratic. Old rules dictated that you should never paint a small room in a dark color, for example. Sometimes, in fact, a dark tone can turn a small room into a jewel box. Harmonious and appropriate color choices depend on a room's use, available natural light, the style of the house, its architecture, the mood of the room, the landscape, the location, and the history of the region.

Colors that are beautiful in California light may look too golden, bright, or inappropriate in a Long Island or London interior. A rich limestone/cream tone or elegant gray/taupe that looks luscious and historically correct in a Paris hotel may look muddy, drab, or dull in a San Francisco apartment overlooking the bay.

The light in Los Angeles is a warm apricot color, so blue and gray tend to look cool and flat, and may lack depth. An East Coast beachfront house might need to be cooled down with a dash of crisp, calm white, while a house in Scottsdale or Santa Fe often looks more appropriate with white with a dash of an earth tone like ocher, clay, or umber.

Experiment, be enthusiastic, and approach color as a grand adventure.

I suggest avoiding trendy colors when choosing paint for décor. Fashion hues and bold Prada-esque combinations can be wonderful and witty on a handbag or on sandals, and may even look enticing on a paint chip, but generally they're disastrous on walls. Shocking pink, khaki, mauve, lime, mango, and bright turquoise are chic and exciting on a silk scarf, an Etro shirt, a Paul Smith striped tie, or a cashmere sweater by Lucien Pellat-Finet, but it's probably wise to keep these fresh colors in your wardrobe rather than splashed on your walls. I've been tempted to translate favorite shades from a pale blue Hermès sweater or a chartreuse Charvet scarf to wall paint, but colors that are fun to wear and make you feel good do not always translate well to walls. They can be fun for a while, but they date and become tiresome (and limiting to décor) rather fast. Fad colors fall out of favor, but good

---

Simple Solutions *Opposite:* The kitchen of this Manhattan duplex was remodeled and updated with a minimum of fuss. Rather than tear out the existing pine cabinets, which had darkened over time, Michael Smith painted them Benjamin Moore's China White. The result: a refreshed yet traditional kitchen that remains true to the original elegance of the apartment.

wall paints should not.

It's often a process of trial and testing, but I try to start with the best choice, not a wild guess.

I've designed and chosen paint for almost every style of room and I've learned over time to be incredibly cautious and seldom to take chances. I test, view, review, and judge the paint and its effect. I might start with four or five great celadon colors to test, or three or four similar cream tones, and paint swatches on the wall to see which one looks best in that location.

Even white, that most basic of all colors, can be very tricky and can easily have the wrong cast and effect. There are hundreds—perhaps thousands—of different whites. Some whites look pale green in certain lights, and have a celadon cast in an ivory room, while others have too much yellow or pink or may appear ashen or overly bright, and too chilly.

I have spent hours on many projects patiently testing cream tones, to find the one that is best suited to the intended use. We compare, we discuss, and we look at our favorites at various times of day. We may find the color needs to be

richer or softer, or perhaps paler or whiter. In the end, the paint must balance and complement all the other tones of fabrics, woods, and carpet, and must make a pleasing composition and background with furniture and art.

I recommend trying four or five samples, as it is almost impossible to get the color right the first time around. For a felicitous result, I make an initial selection of paint colors and discuss the choices with my clients. Wall paints require a great deal of thought—you can't "call it in" or do it by rote. I don't have standard colors I use over and over; each time is different. The color has to be perfect. It's a worthwhile investment to paint swatches, which sometimes lead you to a surprising decision. It's great to discover a rich, luscious, and complex new shade of white or parchment or cream.

I prefer "no-name" colors and "off" colors that are not too specific and have a lot of complexity to ones that are one-dimensional. If a paint is "pale creamish white with just a hint of ocher" or "softest celadon with a touch of clay," or "taupe that's warm with a slight cream cast," then it's going in

For Mood and Memory *Above:* Rich red tones can add surprising depth and richness to a dining room or a family room. Michael Smith often treats red tones in all their variety, as a neutral background for antiques, marble, carved wood paneling, and paintings. Here he used Farrow & Ball's Eating Hall Red paint, a complex terra-cotta–hued matte paint with great depth of color. The English-style "James" dining chair is from the Michael Smith Collection. *Opposite:* Gary and Maria Mancuso Gersh's library has mahogany paneled walls by architect Paul Williams. The ceiling was painted a custom persimmon color to balance the room and to add warmth and drama in the evening light.

the right direction.

Colors that you can instantly describe—bubble-gum pink, plain beige, unmodulated emerald, or plain grayed-down charcoal, for example—are not complex or layered enough for me. They're boring. I want complexity, mystery, and charm. I like a satisfying color that makes you feel good because it's the perfect shade for your room, looks ideal in your special light, and is flattering to you.

CINEMATIC INSPIRATION

I often look to movies—especially those with great art direction and production styles, and attention to historic accuracy—for color ideas.

Camille Claudel, with Isabelle Adjani as the sculptress/lover of Auguste Rodin, has lush taupe and blue tones, and superb cinematography, which emphasizes the marble sculptures and paled-down Paris interiors.

Orlando was shot in some of the great historic interiors of England, and has rich, saturated colors.

Interiors, by Woody Allen, has elegant white and pale blue interiors and superbly controlled color.

Other films that offer a great sense of authenticity and have a feeling or authority on color include *Room With a View* (Florence in a golden light, at its best), *The Mission* (sparse yet rich South American interiors and intense, earthy colors), *The Leopard* (fantastic Sicilian palazzo interiors and beautiful examples of creamy, sunlit rooms), and *House of the Red Lantern* and *The Last Emperor*, which have breathtaking yellows and reds, and use the historic Chinese settings to dazzling and memorable effect. They both demonstrate with bold theatricality, that a dash of pure Imperial yellow, or a touch of intense red, can make a room exciting and give a color scheme a vibrant energy.

GREAT PAINTS

My favorite paint companies are Farrow & Ball (for their historic paint colors), Pratt & Lambert (rich, historically based colors), and Benjamin Moore (for versatile, natural, and pleasing colors).

I also like to use Donald Kaufman Color Collection paints. He's an artist and a colorist, and he mixes paints that are complex, luminous, beautiful, reliable, and very pleasing to the eye. They're couture colors. While most commercial paint colors have at most four or five pigments mixed into the base color to attain the hue, Donald Kaufman uses a full spectrum of as many as twelve pigments, for a mutable and often surprisingly rich color. Even his most neutral colors look multilayered and very elegant. They also change during the

day, so you never get bored with them. They can add a lot to the feeling and mood of a room.

I'm also constantly in pursuit of new paints. I research paints in Europe and carry around swatches of Belgian and French paints for their historic references and subtle tones. I recently discovered a Los Angeles company called Sydney Harbour Paint Company, which makes a variety of paint finishes, lime washes, and intriguing colors. I also like the Fine Paints of Europe collection, including Martha Stewart's colors for the company.

These paints may seem expensive, but the saturated colors, deep pigments, elegant shades, and lasting quality are worth it. With paint, it is always wise to select the best quality possible as your walls will require fewer coats and will be more resistent to wear and tear.

Occasionally, for a guest room or a hallway, we may select Martha Stewart for Kmart paints, which are well priced. We've used Kmart's "Tortilla," which is a very good, rich neutral cream.

I suggest also checking all the different formulations, textures, and types of paints. Colors are available in hundreds of finishes ranging from lime wash, milk paint, distemper, acrylic, eggshell, and French wash, to ultraflat acrylic and satin and semigloss and more. Getting the finish right is as important as getting the color right. Test your selected paint color in one or two different finishes to see which one works best. In general, however, I prefer matte finish walls. Semigloss rather than gloss is usually preferable for woodwork.

SELECTING THE HUE

I gather up small pots of the paint colors (perhaps six to eight) in tones and textures that look promising, and paint large swatches on the walls. Paint companies offer sample pots for as little as $3. They are an excellent investment. Little dabs of postage-stamp samples do not work.

I may base a selection on tones in an antique carpet, or those found in nature. I may be inspired by natural woven silk, leaves, a historical document, or an ancient fresco. Historic colors, or paint colors derived from a room in a painting by John Singer Sargent, for example, have stood the test of a century of two, so they will not date.

I often look to historically correct colors. For my house in Los Angeles, which was inspired by the English country houses of Edwin Lutyens, one of the great British architects of the early twentieth century, I visited residences in the English countryside designed by Lutyens, and studied his palette. It was often based on raw stone, earth, and other natural materials. I worked with Farrow & Ball colors that reflect the style of Lutyens, because they have a soft matte finish

Green Can Be a Neutral *Opposite:* For a Santa Monica cottage, Smith chose Adam-style green paint as a foil for a pair of parcel-gilt neoclassical Scandinavian chairs from Therien & Co. This green, neoclassical favorite, feels fresh and cool on a hot summer day, but its tone is complex to avoid a cold cast.

and a faded look of age that worked perfectly with the new architecture.

SELECTION

After applying a selection of paint hues to the wall, my clients and I look at these big 3- or 4-foot squares in a range of lights. We compare the effects of the colors. I bring in large swatches of the fabrics for curtains and hold them up against the paint, and we look at flooring samples. We never rush the selection. We may even try a few more custom-mixed paint samples, after eliminating several of the initial choices.

One mistake many people make is to choose a color that is not complex enough. Some pale neutral colors look bland, or too bright. Others are just not very interesting or individual. For that reason, I never paint walls plain stark white. It can look too institutional, too cold.

Don't fall for the romance of paint color names. A poetic or witty name—Surf, Cashew, Peanut Brittle, Cloud, Dream, Princess Tiara, Fog, and other names paint companies dream up—may sound charming but they often don't live up to the promise and look utterly uninteresting. Ignore the name, work with the color.

To make a room feel balanced and comfortable, I prefer not to have too much contrast between the wall paint and a door or window frame, or the baseboard. These wood trims should feel harmonious with the wall, rather than competing with it or standing out too strongly.

Colors for trim are challenging. It's hard for the eye to adjust to an abrupt contrast between a wall color and baseboards or a crown molding, so I seldom use a white paint for trim or for millwork, and certainly never a glossy paint. It's often too much of a disparity and too graphic. A soft cream or off-white is often better.

Painting a kitchen or bathroom millwork (wood trim, moldings) in a white or limestone color that's too far from the color of the tile floor or the stone floor can be jarring. Match the wall color to other surface materials, such as the tile.

Drama with paint can be overplayed. Dark and bold colors may seem sumptuous, sexy, and dramatic, but they can also rather swiftly become oppressive, too theatrical and heavy. Dark cigar brown can be tempting for a study, but if it's too deep or dull it can make a room feel closed-in and uninviting. A dark plum color, which might appear to be an original choice, can be dreary and drab in both daylight and at night.

TAKING A CHANCE

Taking risks is admirable, but requires a strong point of view. I do advocate testing and experimenting. That spirit requires the time and budget to repaint again and again, but it is often worth the effort.

There should be leaps of faith with colors, and chances taken. Bravery, frivolity, and confidence can lead to amazing results. I've painted a ceiling in the hallway of a Spanish-style house a deep red; it's magical. In a Montecito Mediterranean-style house, I painted a ceiling pale turquoise. It's a lovely, unexpected detail.

I've become more adventurous as I've gone forward with some clients and for myself. In a modernist penthouse in Santa Monica where I lived a few years ago, I felt compelled to paint a small 12-foot square study in that chic and iconic Hermès-box orange. I'd just read in a design book that the color most hated by decorators was orange. It spurred me on. I had to try it.

I mixed several different Pratt & Lambert orange colors together to gain more complexity, and applied the paint to the walls. Large windows faced north, and the room had a very sculptural Charles Eames bookcase, and a wonderful nineteenth-century Swedish neoclassical table. It was a great experiment because I saw how much I loved orange, how stimulating and exciting it was. The room glowed like a Chinese lantern at night.

The rest of the apartment had palest cream-white walls and a rather neutral background. This dash of orange, viewed at the end of the hallway, was rich and exclamatory. It was a lively contrast with the rest of the interior. I loved entering the room. It was exciting, thrilling. It was a library, really, a place where I kept books, so I never spent much time there. I still recall it fondly.

I painted one of my offices in Santa Monica with flat mocha walls and an off-white trim, with a pale chalky turquoise ceiling. It was so beautiful, so elegant and soothing. For me, it was great and it was very appropriate to the setting and the architecture.

Some experiments are less satisfying. In another Los Angeles apartment, I painted a living room with "Parakeet" by Pratt & Lambert. It's a bright acid green. It was cheerful and modern, and I tempered it with blue and white fabrics, blue-and-white porcelains, and bold antiques. In the end, it was too stimulating, too strong. The color shrieked, and I redid the room in softer greens and off-white. The green concept was right, but it had to be a more subtle, softer version of green.

Colors that are strong and saturated might be too bold

The Freshness of Pale Green *Opposite:* Smith specified a cooking apple green—as fresh as a Regency green—for this entrance hall. It is pale, and a fine foil for a richly gilt Regency-style mirror, and a painted demi-lune console table.

for most people. A rich color like deep moss might work, whereas hot and rich yellow can be too stimulating for a room that needs to be restful, like a bedroom.

I'm always curious to experience certain paint effects. I painted one of my bedrooms a deep tomato red. It was too much, too strong, too intense, practically radioactive. I had thought that it would look rich and sensual and warm, but instead it was like being in the middle of a ripe tomato. Nothing could save it. Experiment over. I painted it out, and started again with pale moss. My eyes needed a rest.

A neutral color need not be bland. For a guesthouse in Montecito, I chose St. Edmunds Beige by Pratt & Lambert. It's a beautiful taupe that alone would have been rather staid. I designed curtains in pale peony–colored pink Sargent Silk, from my fabric collection for Cowtan & Tout. The curtains are unlined, luminous, and romantic

against the taupe background; they look a little Japanese, elegant against the flat taupe walls.

EXTERIOR

I recommend using the same slow process of testing and observing when painting exterior walls and woodwork and doors, as well. Paint large swatches, wait, watch.

It can be a mistake to select a bright white for a clapboard house, or to paint colorful trim on a stucco house. Bright or light colors that look interesting and appropriate on a paint sample can be too bright or too light when hit by sunlight. On the other hand, flat, dull colors can make a house look small, insubstantial, and lifeless. Dull greenish paints can make a house disappear into the foliage.

Test some large swatches of paint on a wall that's in full sun. Check the effect from a distance, against the back-

Colors for Pleasure *Above:* Michael Smith custom-mixed the pale-pink/terra-cotta–toned paint for the wall of a guesthouse loggia in Montecito. "In this country setting, the pale pink tones and the Arles blue window frame look cheerful and a little startling, but charming," said the designer.

ground of trees, or flowers in bloom, or the pool. The result should be harmonious, soothing, and timeless. The house should look "at home" in the landscape. Colors should often be toned down to feel appropriate to the neighborhood. I prefer softer colors that are not overly assertive with the landscape, or too much of a contrast with the setting.

For a modernist house, classic white may be too stark and may make the architecture appear boxy and awkward. It may look too jarring, too bright. Experiment with a softer white, a cream/white or a white with a hint of palest green. The house will look white, but will settle in among the trees and into the landscape harmoniously.

Take into consideration, too, the sheer scale of the exterior and the effect of the paint on a two-story house. The larger the house, the more natural and toned down the paint should be.

COLOR CONFIDENCE

In the end, there are no rules which apply to all walls, to all houses, all locations.

The effect of light and shade, the size and aspect of the room, and a homeowner's taste all suggest the right direction. Test and experiment with several colors before embarking on the complicated and often expensive process of layering on paint indoors or outdoors, and getting the perfect finish.

Consider investing in the best quality paints you can afford. Custom-designed paints can be a terrific investment. Some paint companies suggest that beautiful paints can add ten percent or more to the value of a house. That may have some truth to it. In any case, beautiful colors simply make you feel and look great, and create a comfortable and pleasing atmosphere.

Above: In Smith's former penthouse apartment in Santa Monica, he experimented with matte orange paint, the color of the iconic Hermès packaging. "In a small room, this looked like an installation of color, a glowing lantern at the end of the hallway," he said. "The paint color was certainly decorative and a little shocking. It was a great test, and it worked because the mirror and tables and chairs were boldly scaled and drew the eye. It was certainly dramatic."

SLEEPING BEAUTY

Good beds come in many guises. I've created sumptuous gilt and painted beds, opulent beds with glamorous tufted headboards and pure white linen sheets, beautifully austere Shaker-style four-poster beds with hand-woven blankets, sexy beds with Balenciaga-beautiful pale gray taffeta draperies and plain white cotton sheets, and antique Anglo-Indian beds with elaborate hand-carving dressed with ivory linen sheets. I style each bed differently, often with antique textiles or handcrafted blankets to give it an individual character. For example, in a Montecito, California, guesthouse, I draped an elegant four-poster bed with vivid Shakrishabz and Uzbek antique hand-stitched *suzani* bedcovers.

Yet, all good beds have some qualities in common: character, charm, beguiling style, personality, and great comfort.

Everyone wants a bedroom that's both beautiful and personal.

If possible, I prefer to work on a room with refined and elegant architecture. If balanced interior architecture and detailing are not possible (in a new apartment or loft, for example), I may wallpaper the walls and cornice or cover the walls with fabric to give an illusion of fine proportions and a feeling of dimension. Or I may install a four-poster bed, which can instantly provide a sense of architecture to a room otherwise lacking those qualities; both the room and the bed gain importance and stature. Four-posters work in smaller rooms, as well as grand bedrooms. They become the focal point of the room, radiating a feeling of harmony.

A bedroom should be designed primarily for sleeping and relaxing, and for escaping the noise and rush of the day. It should not do double duty as an office, gym, or media

---

The Many Virtues of a Poster Bed *Opposite:* "Four-poster beds are like a piece of architecture within each room," noted the designer. "They also enclose the sleeper with a feeling of comfort and privacy." The draped bed was crafted in the English style by Sotheby's Restoration. The patchwork bedcover was made from fragments of eighteenth-century French quilts. *Above:* In a forties Beverly Hills house, Michael Smith designed a graceful bed with a clean-lined, modern feeling as a contrast to the curved silhouettes of a caned chair and an upholstered bench.

Views of Manhattan *Following pages:* Smith designed a straightforward bed with a simple walnut headboard for this New York apartment, situated near The Museum of Modern Art. The night tables and bed are in the Michael Smith Collection. The sheets and shams in both cotton and linen are from the Nancy Koltes Collection.

center. Nor should it be an all-purpose family gathering spot. It should feel calm, composed, and well-organized. It must be a room that's magical to sleep in; it should not be cluttered or over-designed.

The essentials of a well-designed bedroom include fresh flowers; a comfortable bed; a good reading light or two; art and antiques you love, and possibly a fireplace; side tables with drawers and shelves for books; a top-quality sound system along with a concealed television and DVD player; curtains or shutters for managing the light; and wonderfully comfortable chairs. It sounds like a lot, but I also like to see family photographs, a place for a telephone, and if possible a chaise longue or sofa. On the other hand, I also like bedrooms that are rather spare, almost monastic. The point is to make it the room you like to come home to, a place of repose and rest.

The room should feel personal and relaxed, but beauty and pleasure can be created in many styles. I would never recommend overly elaborate curtains or vivid satin sheets,

which make a room look vulgar, or matched bedroom sets, which make a room look like a furniture showroom.

For me, an inviting bedroom means freshly pressed white or ivory linen or cotton sheets and a fresh and lofty duvet, along with all the blankets and pillows you need for comfort. I also like bed linens in pale cream, pink, palest blue, and ivory, which can be mixed to great effect.

Décor that is trying too hard to be cool and hip, with hard-edged beds or iconic modern furniture, usually misses by a mile. In the rush to be trendy, it is impersonal and lacking in irony.

For some people, a beautiful bedroom is very simple, with luxurious bedcovers and ethereal white curtains—a pure and calm room that's well-planned and full of promise.

For others, a romantic and sensual bedroom style can be revved up with floral wallpaper and lighthearted antique painted cabinets and chairs, with an elaborate canopied bed as a celebratory centerpiece. I also have some longtime clients who prefer a subdued, tailored room with a Zen

Restful Backgrounds, Bold Antiques *Opposite:* In the master bedroom of a house near Santa Barbara, the bed is positioned in a curtained niche. The nailhead-decorated antique Spanish trunk provides storage for blankets and pillows. *Above:* Antique Spanish chairs and gilt antique Spanish headboards add texture and a sense of delight and luxury to a small room.

mood, crafted with the most understatedly luxurious fabrics and materials.

A lighthearted room full of sunshine and fresh air can be very sexy. Bedrooms that open onto gardens and terraces and trees full of birdsong are wonderful. Imagine being able to start the day by throwing open the windows and doors to a garden.

In the various apartments and houses in which I've lived over the last two decades, I've designed a wide variety of beds and bedrooms. I'm not a devout modernist, so in an all-white seventies penthouse near the beach in Santa Monica, I dressed my steel four-poster with yards of dove-gray shot-silk taffeta, which draped around me as I slept. The bedcover was first a colorful Samarqand *suzani*, and later a rich silk ikat quilt made from a remnant of a Persian court garment.

MAKING THE BED

Mattress choices are very personal. Some of my clients like Duxiana beds; others like custom-made McRoskey Airflex mattresses; still others prefer mattresses made with ecologically correct organic cotton, or pillow-top mattresses made to precise specifications. I propose a "test drive" before buying or ordering to make sure the mattress is neither too firm (there should be some "give" and a sense of comfort and softness) nor too soft (the body needs support and the mattress should have long-lasting and durable structure).

I do have one rule for sheets: no polyester or synthetics whatsoever. Personally, my bed has to be impeccable with white or ivory linens, a handsome wool or cotton blanket, and

Balancing a Bed *Opposite:* A monumental-scale Anglo-Dutch-style bed, bought at auction in New York, creates a sense of imposing stature in this bedroom. The night tables are English antique writing desks, large in scale to balance the bold drama of the carved bed. The walls were painted a pale straw color to give the bed its due prominence.

perhaps a light-as-air Scandinavian down duvet. It must be pure linen and cotton, with no "wrinkle-free" finishes or synthetic fibers. Cotton and linen sheets, freshly washed and ironed, are among life's great luxuries. In hot weather, that's all you need for a blissful night's sleep. In cold weather, with layers of comforters and blankets, cotton sheets feel smooth and uncomplicated.

I prefer sheets and pillowcases to be plain, not patterned. I'm especially partial to linens by Nancy Koltes, Frette, the Company Store (high-thread count sheets and some very luxurious duvets), and the Premiere Collection by Target (in white, of course). Scandia Down makes very luxurious and long-lasting duvets. I like the summer-weight duvets for their lightness and versatility.

Cream or white sheets are versatile, as is a pale blue heathered sheet. Colorful Porthault and Pratesi fine cotton sheets with hearts and flowers on a white background are charming and lighthearted and have a European flavor. Woven stripes in pale blue on white, or ivory on white, can look very crisp and smart. Recently, I've been buying white linen sheets that are hand-embroidered in Morocco. Antique white linen sheets with embroidery can look beautiful and romantic, and they're wonderfully soft to the touch. A discreet monogram can also be perfectly appropriate.

I don't care for overly designed beds with pyramids of pillows or elaborate bedcovers. That's just not sexy; it's all too much work to manage and maintain.

In California, I don't always use a blanket, but in New York or for clients in Montana or Connecticut, I would select a cashmere or alpaca blanket, or a cashmere and silk blend.

Chinese Influences *Opposite:* A theatrical bed, with its gilding and chic coloring, was inspired by a John Linnell original from Badminton House, and now in the collection of the Victoria & Albert Museum in London. "I wanted to make a really dramatic bed for this well-appointed guest room," noted Smith. "The color and drama might be too much to sleep in every night, but it makes a weekend guest feel very special." The bedcover is antique Chinese embroidered silk.

Quilts and matelasse bedcovers are visually pleasing, and offer lightweight warmth.

Many people like to sleep in California King–sized beds. They're a difficult proportion in a room because they're such big, long beds. Dress them simply and without great elaboration so that they don't become too fussy or emphatic.

A four-poster frame around a king-sized bed gives this large object a better proportion because it elevates it and refines its silhouette. The posts make it more magical and interesting; it becomes a room within a room.

I've designed beds with handmade Provençal quilts, with pajama-stripes and Turkish quilts, or with a glamorous shot-silk taffeta duvet cover in pale blue tones. Indian hand-blocked cotton quilts and a white-on-white jacquard duvet cover may be all the pattern you need. But you can't go wrong with white. It's classic, it never dates, and white sheets enhance all décor—and doesn't keep you awake with wild pattern.

You can't beat an all-white bed with beautifully pressed, pristine linens. It looks so inviting and welcoming. You want to jump right in and take a nap.

Forty winks or seven hours of heavenly overnight sleep—sweet dreams and blissful sleep are the ultimate goal of great bed design.

California Comforts *Opposite:* Smith designed this bedroom for a ranch house in the hills above Los Angeles. The fruitwood sleigh-style bed was crafted by Grange.

BEAUTIFUL WINDOWS

Exquisite and elegant curtains define a room. In Bel-Air, I designed couture curtains with two layers of mandarin and lemon matte silk taffeta, which shimmer and glow as the light changes and breezes catch the luxurious fabric. In another house in the Hollywood Hills, I designed utterly simple bedroom curtains made from 200 yards of pure white medium-weight Italian linen with a matte satin finish, hung with a glamorous drape from plain wrought iron rods. The effect, as windows were opened to the garden and a light breeze captured the linen, was as theatrical as the unforgettable ballroom scene in Visconti's *The Leopard* when Sicilian breezes lifted the full-length ivory linen draperies which billowed like ball gowns in the golden summer afternoon light.

I am known for spare, elegant curtains. They're luxurious and beautifully made, but they are subtle. Curtains should not become the focal point of the décor. They should enhance the room, not overwhelm it. Many designers use curtains to make a statement, but I find that windows are often the most overdesigned elements of a room. I prefer to give a feeling of luxury by using the same fabrics and same style of curtain in a series of rooms. It's very beautiful (and very European) to see a series of full curtains in an enfilade of rooms, perhaps going down a long hallway, or in a connecting dining room and living room. It gives the rooms coherence and makes the rooms seem bigger.

Window design should be connected to the architecture of a room, and must be appropriate to the scale, detail-

---

Light as Air *Opposite:* More than 100 yards of fine linen sateen by Rogers & Goffigon were used to make these dreamy curtains for a Portuguese-style quinta in Southern California. They are hung on simple hand-forged rods with discreet oval-shaped finials, and straightforward and efficient steel rings. "These curtains were designed to be elegant and practical, in a manner that is romantically reductive," said the designer. On a hot summer day, they are as fresh as a breeze. *Following pages:* For a ballroom-sized living room in Los Angeles, Michael Smith chose bold and glamorous orange and sharp yellow matte silk taffeta for a series of luxurious curtains. "I don't like shiny silk taffeta for curtains in Los Angeles," said the designer. "At night, it is so reflective and too shiny." The curtains hang on unpretentious mahogany rods with gilt rings.

ing, style, and intention of the architecture.

Curtains should be light enough to float in the breeze, to modify sunlight, and to enhance the décor. Avoid curtains that weigh down the windows or make the room feel heavy and closed in.

I prefer a lightweight curtain with some transparency, a certain weight and body, and an interesting, pleasing texture: linen-and-wool blends, classic pure linen, or silk-and-linen work well because of their surface texture and weight. These natural fabrics are durable, hang beautifully, and appear rich and opulent without being overdone.

I usually select humble woven fabrics in natural fibers, but I make them look lush, not monastic. The key is to use a very generous yardage of simple fabrics. When the fabric and design are understated, the curtains must be generously made, rather than skimpy or stingy-looking.

In general, I prefer curtains to be a classic length, just touching the floor. They should not be too short, or they will look as if they shrank, yet, they also must not be overly long. Droopy, gathered curtains look dated and seem to drag the room down. As for curtains that "pool" and "puddle," that concept now looks ridiculous and exaggerated— the opposite of elegance. These curtains act like dust catchers and make a room appear dowdy.

WINDOW-DRESSING STRATEGIES

I can certainly create elaborate curtains when they're right for a room, but I think understatement is wiser. I am not a big fan of valances, pelmets, or jabots. Don't try too hard.

My advice is to treat curtain-making like couture. It is worth it to pay more for superb craftsmanship. I work with curtain ateliers who use old-world methods and techniques but without fuss or pretension. It's a European approach, and it has many advantages.

Curtains should be rather tailored and clean-looking, never shiny or dramatically patterned. That's why wool can look so delicious. It has a natural matte finish but the fibers

Classic Glamour *Opposite:* Two colors of triple-weight matte silk taffeta from Silk Trading Company create lighthearted curtains in a Los Angeles living room. "This is a youthful way to give couture detail for a young family," noted the designer. The photograph is by Slim Aarons.

and weaves have some substance and presence.

It's important that the curtains are harmonious with the room, but they must also frame the landscape visible through the windows. In a Manhattan duplex overlooking the East River, I designed matte pearl-gray Thai silk curtains with sheer wool Roman shades underneath. The color of the curtains changed from pale and luminous in the early morning light to pearlescent and rich later in the day. They were simple, yet glamorous.

Also take into account the natural light in a room. I like rooms to feel light and airy, not shrouded in fabric. Let in as much light as possible; don't weigh the room down, making it dark and dreary. Keep it lighthearted and fresh: touchable, moveable, and modern.

For a dark room in a house in Beverly Hills, I chose a vanilla-colored light wool layered with yellow wool

---

Elegant Solutions *Above:* To resolve an awkwardly sized bay window, Smith designed side curtains and Roman shades in the same linen/wool fabric in a neutral pale taupe color. The "Ruffino" bench, from the Michael Smith Collection, is covered in antiqued leather. *Opposite:* Bright red Thai silk, unlined and simply styled, gives a warm cast and a theatrical jolt to a modern, art-filled room in Los Angeles. "Don't be afraid to use strong color in a modern room," advised Smith. "It counterbalances sculptures, twentieth-century furniture, and graphic art, and in this case stands up confidently against the steel-framed French doors."

behind it. The design had the effect and warmth of sunlight. It's a traditional French concept to get additional light and reflection into a room.

Some of my clients ask me about electronically operated curtains, but I like the romantic idea of drawing the curtains in the evening, or opening the curtains in the morning to greet the day. I don't like trickery or hidden pulleys or over-scaled rings or rods. I prefer to see all the workings, the simple, age-old mechanics that have worked so well for centuries.

I recently designed a mid-weight cream linen curtain with a vermicelli-like thin bamboo shade underneath. It created a simple and elegant lantern effect at the window, and was very effective to temper the light. For light control in a bedroom, I prefer automatic shades to blackout curtains, which are heavy and dark during the day. Shades disappear during daylight and do not detract from the trans-

parency of the curtains.

While I often work with neutral colors for curtains, I have also used red wool in a study, and a tangerine linen-and-silk blend in a living room. There's something very Old Master about faded green or deep red curtains. They have a subtle, shorthand, historic mood. I'm inspired by curtains in Vermeer's paintings and other interiors painted by the Dutch and Flemish masters. The curtains were substantial to keep out the cold, but not fussy, often featuring just a straightforward flat tape along the edge.

Choose simple curtains made from big helpings of the best fabrics to give the curtains depth. It's all about the drape, lush fullness, and romantic simplicity. Good curtains are so satisfying, so pleasing to the eye. Like a couture gown, much of the luxury is hidden in the expensive construction, but it will give pleasure for years to come.

Indoor, Outdoor *Above:* In the pool house at James and Debbie Burrows's Los Angeles residence, Smith designed curtains in a striped linen by Rogers & Goffigon. The designer is fond of stripes: they offer a sense of pattern without graphic distraction or complication. *Opposite:* For Peter and Megan Chernin's loggia overlooking a swimming pool, the designer selected pale khaki Sunbrella outdoor fabric for curtains, and trimmed tiebacks and borders made from marine blue Sunbrella fabric.

FLOWERS IN INTERIORS

My taste in flowers has evolved over time. I used to like any flowers indoors—as long as they were white. Now I like simply arranged fresh magnolias, tulips, roses, Regale lilies, jasmine, gardenias, white orchids, branches of apple blossom, and delphiniums, in white as well as pastels and muted colors. I love all flowers, as long as they look natural and not too "done." I like the elegant look of exotic orchids in vintage terra-cotta pots, as well as vivid orange and pink poppies and armfuls of garden roses. I recommend avoiding hotel-style floral arrangements and gimmicky flower-vase pairings in favor of graceful and slightly wild flowers.

I've always enjoyed visiting flower shops and markets to see what's fresh and to get ideas. Florists in Antwerp and Paris are full of inspiration and surprises because they take a more sensual and seasonal approach. In spring their stalls will be filled with jonquils, big branches of mimosa, and quince blossom, along with many varieties of daffodils and lilacs. In early summer they'll display once-blooming roses.

European florists also open your eyes to the possibilities of great arching stalks of flowering fennel, sheaves of fresh wheat, or tangles of white or purple clematis. There you also see the beauty of terra-cotta pots full of lavender plants, lilies of the valley, and herbs.

Ideally, we'd all have cutting gardens and greenhouses full of rare orchids, and we could simply bring the best of the season into the house. Well, few of us do, but we can still get that look. I select garden roses rather than long-stemmed, avoid chrysanthemums at all times (the French associate them with death), and I dislike overcultivated flowers, such as rubrum lilies, red roses, and sunflowers.

Even a last-minute bunch of lilies, hydrangeas, or roses brought home after work from the corner grocery or the market can look fresh. I recommend trimming and rinsing the stems, clipping off bruised leaves, and then simply placing the flowers into a glass cylinder with lots of fresh water. Flowers lift your spirits.

Season's Beauty *Above:* Lynn de Rothschild's rather traditional but superbly understated dining table setting, in her family's Manhattan dining room, includes family silver and crystal, and the sheer pleasure of spring peonies, styled with utter simplicity. *Opposite:* In a Bel-Air living room, Michael Smith pulled together a striking vignette which includes a marble-topped oak Kentian console and an iconic and collectible Slim Aarons photograph. The heirloom roses, farm-grown near Santa Barbara, were trimmed and then arranged simply in a tall Venetian vase. The reproduction Chinese porcelain pot is from ABC Carpet in New York.

Floral Abundance *Above and Opposite*: Smith's flower credo is illustrated in these five images. He believes it is best (and chicest) to keep flowers mostly monochromatic, always seasonal, and generally very simple and unfussy. Fragrant pastel roses and peonies in antique crystal vases or plain modern glass column vases are among his favorites. He recommends using flowers at their seasonal peak. An abundance of garden roses can offer an extravagantly beautiful tabletop style, and often one or two pale, open roses can be even more beautiful. Orchids (he seldom chooses white) give a sense of romance and exoticism to any room.

It's best to avoid trendy floral designs like curly bamboo or bare branches of curly willow in modern rooms. They look too staged and not at all sensual.

My favorite flowers in Los Angeles and New York are pastel-colored garden roses in early summer, and the most beautiful white or pale pink peonies arranged in a crystal or glass vase to show the stems. I like them to look loose, a bit wild. I often select blooms in bud so that I can see the whole life of the flower, from the first bud to the last petals falling.

I also like green or white hellebores, lily of the valley in a silver julep cup, branches of spring blossoms in a glass cylinder, or a handful of the freshest daffodils in an antique white ironstone pitcher.

Monochromatic flowers, like a bunch of blue or white hydrangeas or a mound of cream roses in a small silver vase, often work best. Fresh flowers have a certain inherent luxury, so I seldom mix them. I simply put them in a crystal or silver vase and let them speak for themselves.

When I lived in New York, I would buy plain wooden flats of paperwhites from floral designer Renny Reynolds. They're cheerful and fragrant.

Among my favorite flowers in late summer are white daisies, pale pink sweet peas, and chocolate cosmos, as well as pastel-colored hollyhocks because they are so old-fashioned and natural. They don't last long, but for a few days they look very charming.

For a dinner party in New York, I filled antique cloisonné bowls with white peonies. They were not too tall, so guests could see over them. I also like to put small silver cups with yellow roses, viburnum, or a yellow lily at each place setting.

In my bedroom, I like to place small garden plants on the bedside table because they last and have a bright, fresh scent. I buy them at the farmer's market and plant them in rustic and mossy antique terra-cotta pots, which I find at Inner Gardens in West Hollywood.

My favorite orchids are odontoglossum, which have tall, arching branches of small, colorful yellow or crimson flowers. Planted in a simple terra-cotta pot (with fresh green moss covering the roots), they look charming, not pretentious, and they last for weeks.

Boston ferns in colorful old majolica pots can look fantastic. They break up the formality of a study and bring a feeling of freshness to a guest room.

When I'm traveling, I always take fresh flowers back to my hotel room. In Paris I visit Christian Tortu's shop on the Left Bank to find deep purple sweet peas, bouquets of fresh herbs, and poppies, as well as his fantastic scented candles, especially "Tomato Leaf."

Natural Beauty *Above left:* In a Malibu Colony beach house, oak branches were arranged for their aura of cool, rustic beauty. The wall paint is by Farrow & Ball. *Below left:* In Peter Morton's modern study in Bel-Air, the designer placed branches of magnolia from the garden in a simple column glass vase. The table is from Carlton Hobbs. *Opposite:* On a painted Gustavian table, a generous gathering of fragrant lilac lift the spirits.

APPRAISING A HOUSE TO BUY
STAGING A HOUSE FOR SALE

I love going to open houses. It's part of my education as a decorator to see what's on the market, and to take a look at houses my clients may be considering. I've learned how to appraise apartments and houses for sale to quickly evaluate their brilliance or their shortcomings, and I've also learned how to stage a house to best advantage when it's time to sell.

APPRAISING A HOUSE TO BUY

I start appraising the moment I arrive at the front door. I do not review the owners' furniture or art. That will go, but the beautiful parquet floor will remain, as will the graceful staircase. I check ceiling heights, and the floor plan to make sure that the rooms have a logical flow. I look at the way light enters, and decide if my furniture will look at home.

I would advise you to visit every house with an open mind, regardless of style. Look at houses at each end of the spectrum—new and old—and view fixer-uppers as well as houses with everything in perfect order. Don't reject a house because the exterior paint is the wrong color.

I look for a sense of authenticity. A house that has never been renovated may need some up dating, but it is almost always a better acquisition than a house that's been so heavily remodeled that all character and soul has been removed.

Check the foundations. I have several friends who started renovations and discovered that foundations were totally inadequate. That's a shock—as are the accompanying months of upheaval and great expense. Ask your realtor for estimates on any required updates or renovations.

Study the location, check parking, know the current and potential property values, and any downside to the location. Find the best realtor you can, and make him or her a confidant.

Stay optimistic. While it's important to "kick the tires" to be sure that everything is solid and well-built, also look for charm, individuality, a sense of peace, and a feeling of security and privacy.

And if you're thinking of making a dramatic move—across country perhaps, or to the country from the city—consider renting for a few months and visiting on weekends.

Color Concepts *Opposite:* Michael Smith prefers classic white bed linens, but in this charming bedroom he liked the freshness and natural charm of blue sheets. A nineteenth-century mahogany bed, Peking glass, striped Cowtan & Tout wallpaper, and a gilded mirror give this room a colorful jolt.

STAGING A HOUSE FOR SALE

When the time comes to sell your home, you can apply the same principles in reverse. The qualities that make a house a wonderful place to live are many of the same qualities that make it compelling to a buyer.

First of all, the house must be pristine, with polished floors, fresh paint, and clean carpets. It's that sense that a house is superbly maintained that will sell it.

To give a tantalizing first impression, the house must smell fantastic. Keep cleaning products natural and fragrance-free so that no chemical smells or over-powering scents linger. Add simply arranged fresh flowers and healthy houseplants. Leave the windows open, and the doors ajar to terraces and patios.

Kitchen cabinets should look neat and clean. I like to see fresh fruit in bowls, potted herbs in the window, and clean towels.

Countertops look best when clutter is removed. Put away children's and pet's toys. Dust off your books, and place magazines neatly in baskets or on side tables.

Plump up the beds, and make them up with fresh sheets and pillowcases. Freshen upholstered chairs and sofas by turning cushions, shaking pillows, and smoothing out lumps and bumps.

Place family photographs out of view. Potential buyers want to imagine themselves in the space.

In bathrooms, neatly stack fresh towels and open fresh soaps with light floral scents.

The yard should be trimmed and tailored. Fill planters with seasonal flowers and herbs. Hoses should be rolled, and garden gates should be painted, with their hinges oiled.

Freshly paint the exterior of your home, using glossy paint for the front door. All hardware should be cleaned and buffed; all wood trim, baseboards, and door frames should be freshly washed down.

Buyers respond to order and perfection in a house. It may be difficult, or impossible, to live like this every day, but this is the way to sell your house for the best possible price.

Artful and Graceful *Above:* Monochromatic flowers, always fresh, make a good impression when potential buyers (and friends) come to look at the house. It's wise not to clutter tabletops, but silver candlesticks, beautiful books, and gleaming surfaces will ooze charm and grace.

Pleasing the Senses *Opposite:* Everything is in its place, and every detail in this fresh-air setting is superbly finessed and polished. Pillows are plumped, a throw awaits, plants are healthy and flourishing. The impression for a visitor, or for a potential buyer, is perfection.

RESOURCES FOR MICHAEL SMITH DESIGNS

KITCHEN AND BATHROOM FITTINGS AND FIXTURES

The Michael S. Smith Collections, For Town, For Country, and For Loft. 1-888-4Kallista and www.kallista.com.

The Michael S. Smith Collection for Ann Sacks. 1.800.278Tile and www.annsacks.com.

FABRIC

Cowtan & Tout
111 8th Avenue, Suite 930
New York, NY 10011
212-647-6900. Phone
212-647-6906 Fax

Jasper Fabric
1646 Nineteenth Street
Santa Monica, CA 90404
Tel. 310.315.3018
Fax. 310.315.3059
info@jasperfabric.com

Fifty-nine fabrics including eight printed designs on hemp, and woven designs in cotton, linen, and cotton-linen blends.

SHOWROOMS
(to the trade)

ASPEN
John Brooks, Inc.
2551 Delores Way
Suite 200
Carbondale, CO 81623
Tel. 970.274.1520

ATLANTA
Ainsworth-Noah
351 Peachtree Hills Avenue
Atlanta Decorative Arts Center
Suite 518
Atlanta, GA 30305
Tel. 404.261.1302

CHICAGO
John Rosselli & Associates
6-158 Merchandise Mart
Chicago, IL 60654
Tel. 312.822.0760

DALLAS
David Sutherland
1025 N. Stemmons Freeway
Suite 340
Dallas, TX 75207
Tel. 214.742.6501

DENVER
John Brooks, Inc.
601 S. Broadway
Suite L
Denver, CO 80209
Tel. 303.698.9977

HOUSTON
David Sutherland
5120 Woodway Drive
Suite 170
Houston, TX 77056
Tel. 713.961.7886

LOS ANGELES
Thomas Lavin
Pacific Design Center
8687 Melrose Avenue
Suite B-310
West Hollywood, CA 90069
Tel. 310.278.2456

NEW YORK
John Rosselli & Associates
979 Third Avenue
Suite 1801
New York, NY 10022
Tel. 212.593.2060

SAN FRANCISCO
Randolph & Hein
San Francisco Design Center
101 Henry Adams Street
Suite 101
San Francisco, CA 94103
Tel. 415.864.3550

SCOTTSDALE
John Brooks, Inc.
2732 N. 68th Street
Suite 1
Scottsdale, AZ 85257
Tel. 480.675.8828

SEATTLE
Nino Serra
5701 6th Avenue South,Suite 105
Seattle, WA 98108
Tel. 206.957.6005

WASHINGTON D.C.
John Rosselli & Associates
1515 Wisconsin Avenue, NW
Washington, DC 20007
Tel. 202.337.7676

FURNITURE AND ACCESSORIES

Michael Smith's furniture and accessories collection includes more than 126 pieces. It is available at the following show-rooms (to the trade):

ASPEN
John Brooks, Inc.
2551 Delores Way
Suite 200
Carbondale, CO 81623
Tel. 970.274.1520

ATLANTA
Ainsworth-Noah
351 Peachtree Hills Avenue
Atlanta Decorative Arts Center
Suite 518
Atlanta, GA 30305
Tel. 404.261.1302

CHICAGO
John Rosselli & Associates
6-158 Merchandise Mart
Chicago, IL 60654
Tel. 312.822.0760

DALLAS
David Sutherland
1025 N. Stemmons Freeway
Suite 340
Dallas, TX 75207
Tel. 214.742.6501

DANIA
John Rosselli & Associates
Design Center of the Americas
1855 Griffin Road
Suite A128
Dania, FL 33004
Tel. 954.920.1700

DENVER
John Brooks, Inc.
601 S. Broadway
Suite L
Denver, CO 80209
Tel. 303.698.9977

HOUSTON
David Sutherland
5120 Woodway Drive
Suite 170
Houston, TX 77056
Tel. 713.961.7886

LOS ANGELES
Thomas Lavin
Pacific Design Center
8687 Melrose Avenue
Suite B-310
West Hollywood, CA 90069
Tel. 310.278.2456

NEW YORK
John Rosselli & Associates
979 Third Avenue
Suite 1801
New York, NY 10022
Tel. 212.593.2060

SAN FRANCISCO
Randolph & Hein
San Francisco Design Center
101 Henry Adams Street
Suite 101
San Francisco, CA 94103
Tel. 415.864.3550

SCOTTSDALE
John Brooks, Inc.
2732 N. 68th Street
Suite 1
Scottsdale, AZ 85257
Tel. 480.675.8828

SEATTLE
Nino Serra
5701 6th Avenue South
Suite 105
Seattle, WA 98108
Tel. 206.957.6005

Opposite: Michael Smith's bathroom and kitchen fittings and fixtures designs for Kohler are inspired and guided by the concepts and designs he uses for his own clients.

MICHAEL SMITH'S FAVORITE RESOURCES FOR ANTIQUES, DESIGN, AND PAINT

NEW YORK CITY

Ann Morris
239 East 60th Street
New York, NY 10022
Tel. 212.755.3308

Beauvais Carpets
201 East 57th Street
New York, NY 10022
Tel. 212.688.2265
www.beauvaiscarpets.com

Carlton Hobbs LLC
60 East 93rd Street
New York, NY 10128
Tel. 212.423.9000
www.carltonhobbs.com

Delorenzo 1950
440 Lafayette Street
New York, NY 10003
Tel. 212.995.1950

De Vera
1 Crosby Street
New York, NY 10013
Tel. 212.625.0838
www.deveraobjects.com

Niall Smith
306 East 61st Street, 5th floor
New York, NY 10012
Tel. 212.750.3985

LONDON

Carlton Hobbs
8 Little College Street
London SW1P 3SH
Tel. 011.44.20.7340.1000
www.carltonhobbs.com

Christopher Hodsoll Ltd
89-91 Pimlico Road
London SW1W 8PH
Tel. 011.44.20.7730.3370

Ciancimino
99 Pimlico Road
London SW1W 8PH
Tel. 011.44.20.7730.9950

Colefax & Fowler
39 Brook Street
London W1K 4JE
Tel. 011.44.20.7493.2231

Godson & Coles
92 Fulham Road
London SW3 6HR
Tel. 011.44.20.7584.2200

Guinevere Antiques
574-580 Kings Road
London SW6 2DY
Tel. 011.44.20.7736.2917

John Hobbs
107A Pimlico Road
London SW1W 8PH
Tel. 011.44.20.7730.8369

Westenholz Antiques Ltd
76-78 Pimlico Road
London SW1W 8PL
Tel. 011.44.20.7824.8090

DESIGN RESOURCES

NEW YORK CITY

ABC Carpet & Home
888 Broadway
New York, NY 10003
Tel. 212.473.3000

Amy Perlin Antiques
306 East 61st Street, 4th floor
New York, NY 10021
Tel. 212.593.5756
www.amyperlinantiques.com

Ann Morris
239 East 60th Street
New York, NY 10022
Tel. 212.755.3308

Antik
104 Franklin Street, Apt 1
New York, NY 10013
Tel. 212.343.0471
www.antik-nyc.net

Beauvais Carpets
201 East 57th Street
New York, NY 10022
Tel. 212.688.2265
www.beauvaiscarpets.com

Cove Landing
995 Lexington Avenue
New York, NY 10021
Tel. 212.288.7597

Delorenzo 1950
440 Lafayette Street
New York, NY 10003
Tel. 212.995.1950

De Vera
1 Crosby Street
New York, NY 10013
Tel. 212.625.0838
www.deveraobjects.com

Gerald Bland Incorporated
1262 Madison Avenue
New York, NY 10128
Tel. 212.987.8505

HM Luther Inc Antiques
61 East 11th Street
New York, NY 10003
Tel. 212.505.1485
www.hmluther.com

HM Luther Incorporated
35 East 76th Street
New York, NY 10021
Tel. 212.439.7919
www.hmluther.com

John Rosselli Antiques
255 East 72nd Street
New York, NY 10021
Tel. 212.737.2252

Magen H Gallery
80 East 11th Street
New York, NY 10003
Tel. 212.777.8670

MD Flacks Ltd
38 East 57th Street, 6th floor
New York, NY 10022
Tel. 212.838.4575

Nancy Koltes Associates
900 Broadway, Suite 201
New York, NY 10003
Tel. 212.979.5664

Nancy Koltes at Home
31 Spring Street
New York, NY 10012
Tel. 212.219.2271

R 20th Century Design
82 Franklin Street
New York, NY 10013
Tel. 212.343.7979

Robert Altman
306 East 61st Street
New York, NY 10021
Tel. 212.832.3490

LOS ANGELES

RM Barokh Antiques
8481 Melrose Place
Los Angeles, CA 90069
Tel. 323.655.2771

Bennison Fabrics Incorporated
8264 Melrose Avenue
Los Angeles, CA 90069
Tel. 323.653.7277

Darcey Herd Custom Florals
Tel. 310.444.9959
dhcustomflorals@earthlink.net

Double Vision
1223 Abbot Kinney Boulevard
Venice, CA 90291
Tel. 310.314.2679

Christopher Farr
748 North La Cienega Boulevard
Los Angeles, CA 90069
Tel. 310.967.0064
www.cfarr.co.uk

Hollyhock
817 Hilldale Avenue
West Hollywood, CA 90069
Tel. 323.931.3400
www.hollyhockinc.com

Inner Gardens Incorporated
8925 Melrose Avenue
West Hollywood, CA 90069
Tel. 310.274.0129

Janus Et Cie
8687 Melrose Avenue, Suite 146
Los Angeles, CA 90069
Tel. 310.652.7090
www.janusetcie.com

JF Chen Antiques
8414 Melrose Avenue
Los Angeles, CA 90069
Tel. 323.655.6310

John Iloulian Rugs
8451 Melrose Place
Los Angeles, CA 90069
Tel. 323.651.0993
www.megerianrugs.com

Kim 3 Asian Art & Antiques
8923 Beverly Boulevard
Los Angeles, CA 90004
Tel. 310.859.3844

Lee Stanton Antiques
769 North La Cienega
Boulevard
West Hollywood, CA 90069
Tel. 310.855.9800

**Mansour Fine Rug & Floor
Covering**
8600 Melrose Avenue
Los Angeles, CA 90069
Tel. 310.652.9999

Paul Ferrante Incorporated
8464 Melrose Place
Los Angeles, CA 90069
Tel. 323.653.4142

Quatrain Incorporated
700 North La Cienega Boulevard
Los Angeles, CA 90069
Tel. 310.652.0243
www.quatrain.net

Reborn Antiques
853 North La Cienega Boulevard
Los Angeles, CA 90069
Tel. 310.289.7785

Robert Kuo Limited
8686 Melrose Avenue
Los Angeles, CA 90069
Tel. 310.855.1555
www.robertkuo.com

Samuel's Rug Gallery
8636 Melrose Avenue
Los Angeles, CA 90069
Tel. 310.657.3666
www.absoluterugs.com

Therien & Company
716 North La Cienega Boulevard
Los Angeles, CA 90069
Tel. 310.657.4615
www.therien.com

PAINT

I like the paint collections by
Donald Kaufman, for their artful colors and the depth of the
hues. And I work with other
companies, selecting always
colors that have complexity,
versatility, and character.

WHITE COLORS
Pratt & Lambert Silver Lining 2288
Pratt & Lambert Seed Pearl 2314
Benjamin Moore China White
Benjamin Moore Monterey White HC-27
(HC=Historic Colors Collection)

COOL COLORS
Farrow & Ball French Grey 18
Farrow & Ball Cooking Apple Green 32
Farrow & Ball Ball Green 75

WARM COLORS
Farrow & Ball Dorset Green
Pratt & Lambert Mission 2121
Pratt & Lambert Italian Straw 1752
Pratt & Lambert Golden Straw 2094
Benjamin Moore Hawthorn Green 379

NEUTRALS
Benjamin Moore
Carrington Beige HC 93
Benjamin Moore Standish White HC 32
Benjamin Moore Seaspray 941
Farrow & Ball Old White 4
Farrow & Ball Off White 3
Pratt & Lambert Silver Blonde 2141
Pratt & Lambert Edmonds Beige 2204
Pratt & Lambert Ceylon Ivory 2101

PHOTOGRAPHY CREDITS

The Glamour Room *Opposite:* Michael Smith decorates bathrooms with antiques, fine rugs, Ann Sacks tiles, Kohler fixtures, and all the other top-quality accoutrements he specifies for other rooms in the house. A bathroom, even a small powder room, should have a sense of luxury, ease, comfort, and originality, he said.

INDEX

ABOUT THE AUTHORS

Diane Dorrans Saeks is the bestselling author of seventeen books on interior design, architecture, décor, and style. Her most recent book is *Hollywood Style*. She is the California Editor of *Metropolitan Home*, and the Interior Design Editor of *PaperCity* and Editor at Large for *C* Magazine. She is also the San Francisco correspondent for *W* magazine, and *WWD*, and contributes to many publications around the world. She lives in San Francisco.

Michael S. Smith, who founded his interior design company Michael S. Smith Inc. in 1990, has become one of the most well-respected and sought-after interior decorators in the country.

Known for his inventive style of mixing Old World classicism with contemporary settings, Smith customizes each project, creating a unique expression that reflects both the client's needs and his own taste.

His style can be called a blend of European tradition and American Modernism. The result is a comfortable elegance, a non-theatrical look that is ultimately very understated in its presentation

In addition to creating a line of reproduction furniture, Smith developed Jasper, his own fabric collection sold exclusively through showrooms around the United States. Additionally, he developed a fabric line for Cowtan & Tout, as well as three distinct lines of bath fixtures for Kallista.

Smith's projects are regularly featured in a number of publications, including *Architectural Digest, Elle Decor, House & Garden, Town & Country, Interior Design, W* and *House Beautiful*, among others.

He has received the Pacific Design Center's Star of Design award, *Elle Decor*'s Designer of the Year honor, and has been named one of the top 100 designers by *Architectural Digest*.

ACKNOWLEDGMENTS

Diane Dorrans Saeks:

Rizzoli publisher Charles Miers and I dreamed up the concept of this book in Los Angeles, inspired by the spirit of inventiveness and creativity of California. I would like to thank Charles for his enthusiasm for this project from the start, and for his insight and wisdom. Kathleen Jayes has been a superb editor, and I have appreciated her fine eye and steady focus. Many thanks also to Ellen Nidy, Pamela Sommers, Jacob Lehman, Paul McKevitt, and his team at Subtitle.

Michael Smith has been an incredibly inspiring, thoughtful, energetic, witty, deft, and amusing partner in this book. We worked on the book as he flew to Jamaica, Brussels, Antwerp, Paris, and London, and I headed for Paris, Tokyo, New York, and Houston (thank you, Cy Twombly, for divine inspiration).

I look forward to working with Michael on the next book project.

Michael Smith:

It's terrific to have a great friend, Diane Dorrans Saeks, with whom I've enjoyed almost seventeen years of telephone conversations, to collaborate with on this wonderful book.

Many thanks to Charles Miers, publisher of Rizzoli, for being such a champion of this book.

Kathleen Jayes has such a fine sense of calm, and has been a meticulous editor.

I have been fortunate enough to work with many talented and passionate photographers. To document my work with them has been exciting and, though often hard work, incredibly rewarding. This book is truly a product of their beautiful work as well as mine.

In addition to keeping my professional life under control and on track against all odds, Sabrina Wrablicz has mastered beautiful air-traffic control with dozens of photographers for this book.

She found unfindable photographs, and finessed ungetable releases in the face of deadlines.

Krista Smith, a longtime friend, observer, and reporter on all things Hollywood, placed my career in the special context of California. A big thank you.

Howard Marks wrote a heartfelt and insightful preface. Howard and Nancy Marks are amazing, supportive, and loving friends.

Many thanks to Margaret Russell. In addition to being a great friend, she helped me immensely with her own knowledge and experiences in publishing.

To all my clients, many thanks and much gratitude. My clients have given me huge amounts of creative freedom, taken great chances, and rewarded me with years of loyalty and friendship. Many of their houses will be in my next book.

Working with me on all these projects are amazing teams of talented professionals who take great pride in their work. Behind every successful decorator, there is a great architect and I owe enormous specific credit to my frequent collaborators, architects Oscar Shamamian and Joseph Singer, as well as Michael Kovac. I appreciate their generosity and vision.

I am fortunate to work with a terrific group of spirited and hard-working people in my office. Most of them have worked with me for many years, and are now part of my extended family.

I especially want to recognize Mark Matuszak, for his incredible talent, friendship, and sense of humor. He has been a constant and joyful collaborator for many more years than either of us would care to admit.

To James Costos. He has encouraged and supported me through every stage of this project, and been incredibly patient through many hours-long Saturday morning phone calls with Diane. James has taught me that there are things more important than decorating.